STANDARD LOAN

Unless recalled by another Reader
this item may be borrowed for

D1756612

Marl

WITHDRAWN

WS 2256695 3

10 / 2005

Printed in Canada

Google Search Marketing: AdWords

Detailed Objectives:

At the end of this lesson, learners should be able to:

- Describe the history and current state of online marketing and advertising

- Compare online advertising and traditional approaches

- Explain how search marketing works

- Contrast organic and sponsored search results on Google

- Identify the parts of an AdWords ad

- Identify Google content network sites and ads

UNIVERSITY OF CHICHESTER

658.
872
900

Online Advertising: A Brief History of a Young Medium

It's safe to say that the Internet has changed the world. It's changed:

- The way we learn
- Find information (search)
- Shop (no need to change out of those pajamas)
- Communicate (email anyone worldwide instantly)

In advertising, the Internet has created a revolution. Online advertising made its debut in October 1994, when HotWired.com began displaying banner ads at the top of web pages. (The first banner ad is shown in Image 1-1.)

Image 1-1: The first banner ad.

Although things started off simply, they soon got rocky for online advertising. Ideas and services quickly saturated the Internet. Expectations ran high. Many start-up companies expected online advertising alone to make them profitable. But in 2001, the dot-com crash squashed many hopes, sending thousands of investors and start-up enterprises into bankruptcy.

After the crash, many online advertising agencies began experimenting with different online advertising models, and online advertising has enjoyed a major resurgence since. Indeed, in its first decade, online advertising revenue grew by leaps and bounds – from just a few hundred thousand dollars per year in 1994 to nearly $10 billion in 2004.

But there were still problems as advertisers tried to learn the best ways to advertise online. For example, annoying pop-up ad frequently covered the content of the page users wanted to read. And then there were pop-under ads–pop-ups appearing underneath webpages, causing users to have to repeatedly close advertising windows they did not want to see in the first place.

Online advertising was at risk of alienating potential customers.

Google Launches AdWords

In 2000, Google launched a keyword-targeted advertising program called AdWords, revolutionizing the online advertising industry. AdWords made search engine marketing (SEM) effective. AdWords showed ads on Google.com that were related to a person's specific search (Image 1-2). And Google disallowed pop-up and pop-under ads of any kind.

More: SEM is also called search advertising or search marketing.

More: The success of AdWords allows Google to provide many free services (including its top-ranked search service). To see (and try out) the full range of free Google services, go to **www.google.com/options/**.

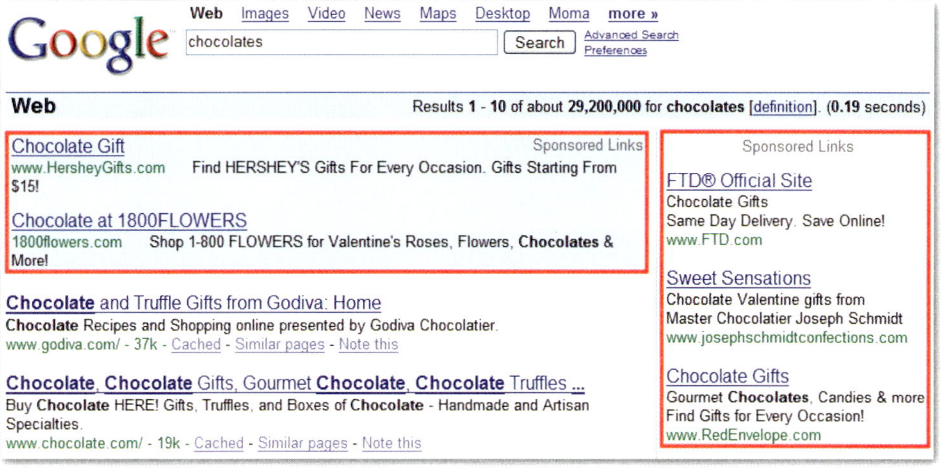

Image 1-2: Google AdWords ads shown on Google.com. Ads are marked with the words 'Sponsored Links.'

Topic 2

Online Advertising Joins the Marketing Mix

In the 20th century, advertisers diversified their advertising across many mediums – such as TV, radio, print, and billboards – to promote their products or services. This diversification is referred to as a **marketing mix**. As people began spending more time online, the Internet became another **channel** via which advertisers can market their goods.

Because of the Internet's versatility, it gives advertisers a good way to reach, engage, and interact with people. Advertisers can produce **campaigns** that specifically **target** audiences more effectively than traditional advertising efforts. Online campaigns give advertisers new abilities to reach:

• Niche markets with specific interests

• Broad audiences with a single message

• Large or small geographic segments

• Speakers of specific languages

As a result of changing consumer habits and advertiser needs, the vast majority of companies now allocate part of their marketing budget to online advertising. It's currently the fastest growing advertising category, as shown in Image 1-3.

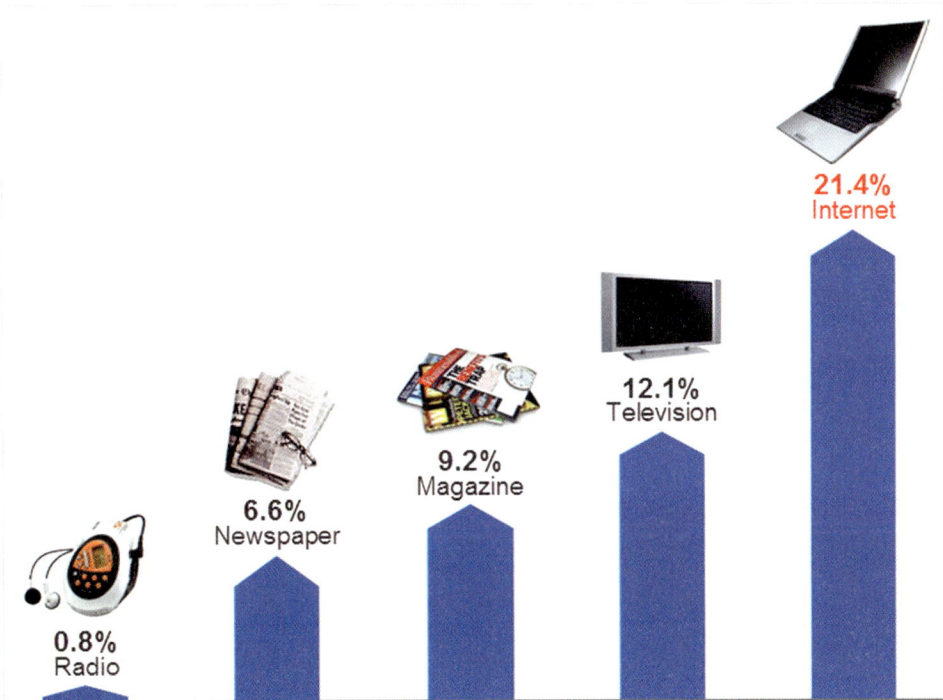

Image 1-3: Change in advertising spend 2005 vs. 2004. Search has been the primary driver of growth in online advertising. (Source: Advertising Age, TNS media intelligence, Universal McCann, June 2005; eMarketer calculations, August 2005)

Successful online marketing campaigns require the application of the three R's of advertising: **reach**, **relevance**, and **return on investment (ROI)**. Online advertising, AdWords in particular, has given advertisers new possibilities in these three areas:

- **Reach:** More than 170 million people use the Internet in the United States. Google's network reaches 80% of these potential customers.
- **Relevance:** AdWords shows ads to potential customers who are actively searching for what businesses have to offer.
- **Return on investment (ROI):** Using analytical tools, advertisers can understand more about the effectiveness of their ads (such as who clicks on them).

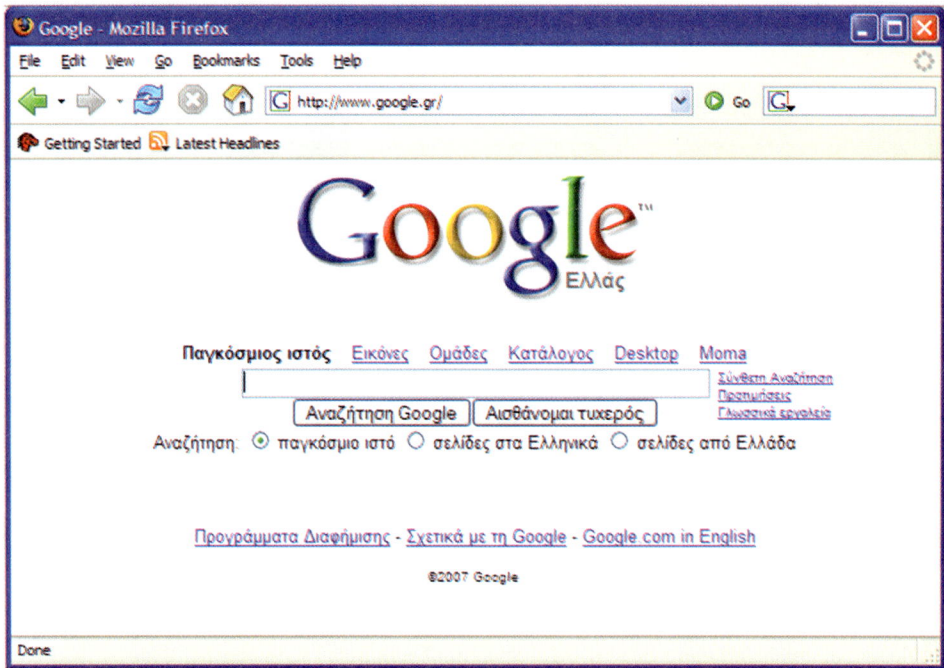

Image 1-4: The reach of AdWords goes well beyond the U.S., spanning the globe. This page is from Greece.

Behind the Scenes: How Google Search Works

Google is the world's most popular search engine. More than 60% of Internet **users** around the world use Google to search for information, products, or services. Google's popularity stems from its minimalist design and the relevancy of its search results.

When a user visits Google.com, he enters a **keyword** and presses the **Google Search button** (this is called a search **query**). In response, Google displays a **search results page**, which lists web pages relating to the search query. The most relevant page appears first, followed by the second most relevant page, and so on.

How does Google know which results are most relevant? The answer lies in Google's **algorithms**, which are a set of advanced calculations that help identify the relevancy of results to each search query. Google **crawls** the web regularly, **indexing** billions of web pages – similar to the way a library card catalog indexes books. When a user enters a search term, Google scans its vast index and displays the most relevant pages based on **PageRank™** and other advanced algorithms.

PageRank™ relies on the link structure of the web as an indicator of an individual page's value. In essence, Google interprets a link from page A to page B as a vote, by page A, for page B. But Google looks at more than the sheer volume of links a page receives; it also analyzes the page that hosts the link. Votes cast by pages that are themselves "important" weigh more heavily and help to make other pages "important."

The technology of search is remarkable. Image 1-3 gives a quick glimpse of what happens when a user performs a query on Google.

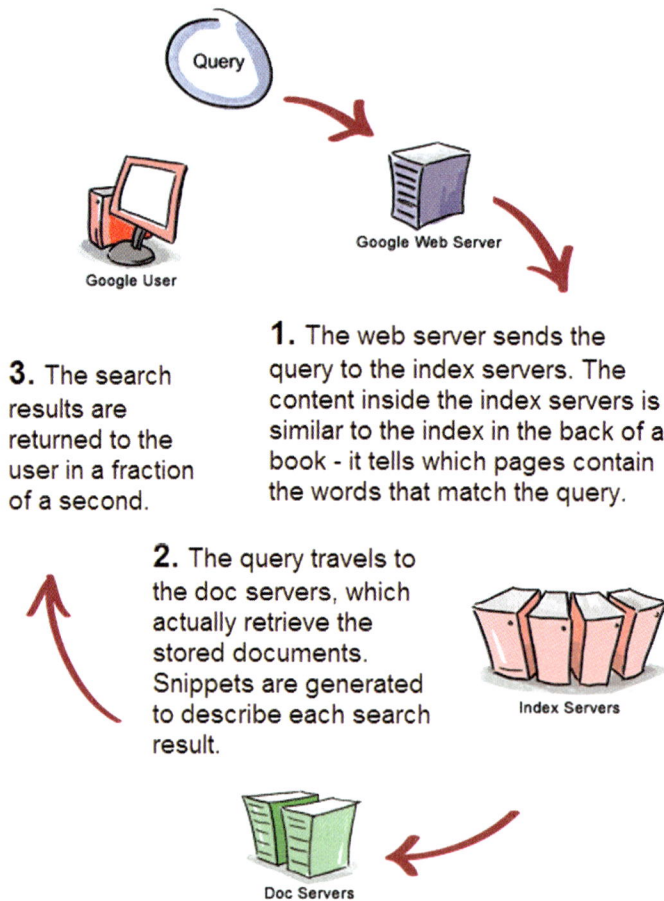

1. The web server sends the query to the index servers. The content inside the index servers is similar to the index in the back of a book - it tells which pages contain the words that match the query.

3. The search results are returned to the user in a fraction of a second.

2. The query travels to the doc servers, which actually retrieve the stored documents. Snippets are generated to describe each search result.

Image 1-5: The life-cycle of a query.

In Image 1-6, you can see a sample **search result** (not an ad) for the keyword "AdWords." Look at the elements more closely:

a) The first line is the title of the web page and a link to the page.

b) The title is followed by a few lines of text that Google pulls from the actual web page. This information is used to help the user deem whether the information on that web page is useful. The actual search query appears in **bold** within the text.

c) The last line shows 1) a web address, called the **uniform resource locator (URL)**, 2) a link to a **Cached** (stored) copy of the information, and 3) a **Similar pages** option.

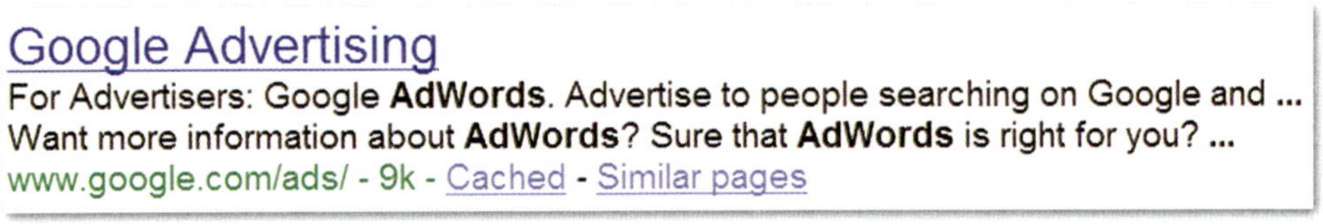

Google Advertising

For Advertisers: Google **AdWords**. Advertise to people searching on Google and ...
Want more information about **AdWords**? Sure that **AdWords** is right for you? ...
www.google.com/ads/ - 9k - Cached - Similar pages

Image 1-6: A Google search result.

Search engine marketing can only work as well as the search engine that supports it. Google co-founder Larry Page has said, "The perfect search engine would understand exactly what you mean and give back exactly what you want." Craig Silverstein, Google's director of technology, has said, "My guess is that in about 300 years computers will be as good as, say, your local reference library in doing search. But we can make slow and steady progress, and maybe one day, we'll get there."

More: Google's corporate mission is to "organize the world's information and make it universally accessible and useful." To accomplish this goal, Google's powerful search system was created. Invented by Larry Page and Sergey Brin in a Stanford University dorm room, Google search allows people from all over the world to pinpoint the information they need, usually in under a second.

Activity 1-1

1. Open your web browser and visit Google.com (Tip: You can omit the www. in **www.google.com**.)

2. Enter "Google advertising" in the search box and click the 'Google Search' button.

3. Scroll through the first 10 or 20 links. List what you believe are the three most relevant links based on your query. Then, write the position in which they appear. (Are they the first, second, seventh?)

First-choice URL: _____

Position on the list: _____

Second-choice URL: _____

Position on the list: _____

Third-choice URL: _____

Position on the list: _____

4. Click the 'Cached' link for your first-choice result. Describe what appears. What do you think the purpose of the 'Cached' link is?

5. Use your browser's back button, and return to your list of results. Click the 'Similar pages' link for your first choice. How relevant are these links to your search query?

6. Visit the following Google search tools in different languages:

- google.de
- google.gr
- google.co.jp
- google.co.uk

7. Notice that on the Google search page for the United Kingdom (google.co.uk), an option appears below the search bar allowing users to view only pages from the U.K. Select this option, and enter the following search term: "Google advertising." What differences do you notice compared to when you entered the same search term into Google.com?

More: What's a Google? "Googol" is the mathematical term for a 1 followed by 100 zeros. The term was coined by Milton Sirotta and was popularized in the book, Mathematics and the Imagination. Google's play on the word reflects the company's mission to organize the immense amount of information available on the web.

Topic 4

AdWords Ads Fundamentals

As mentioned in the previous topic, Google matches highly relevant search results to any search query entered. In addition, Google displays relevant AdWords ads above and alongside search results. These are labeled '**Sponsored Links**,' as seen in Image 1-7. Google separates search results from ads for user distinction.

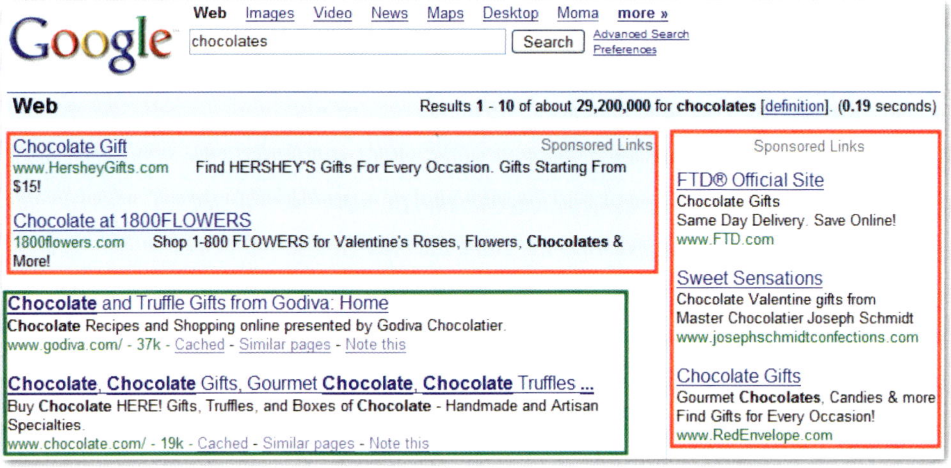

Image 1-7: AdWords ads are placed to the right and sometimes above Google's search results. Organic or natural search results are outlined in green.

Advertisers design AdWords ads to target the user's search (or wants or needs), matching ads to the user's query. Advertisers first choose keywords that relate to their website or product offerings. Then, when a user enters the same or similar keywords into Google, the advertiser's ads are shown. Price and other factors also play a part in ad display (we'll discuss the details later).

As you can see in Image 1-8, there are three main components to an AdWords ad:

1. **Headline:** This is the top line and has a 25-character limit. Usually, it's a quick glimpse at the advertiser's offerings.

2. **Description:** The description follows the headline. It's comprised of two lines of text – each with a maximum limit of 35 characters. (Together with the headline, the top three lines are called the **ad copy**.)

3. **Display URL:** This is the URL that appears at the end of the ad. It identifies which site the user will visit via clicking an ad.

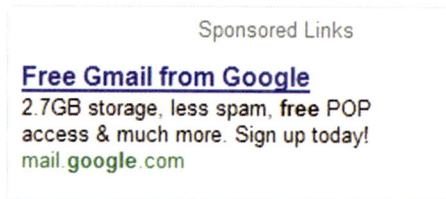

Sponsored Links

Free Gmail from Google
2.7GB storage, less spam, **free** POP access & much more. Sign up today!
mail.**google**.com

Image 1-8: A Google AdWords ad: headline, description and display URL.

Activity 1-2

Like window shopping in the mall, you can window shop online. Try it out to test the results of finding a product you may have purchased in the past:

1. Open your web browser and go to Google.com.

2. Search for any products you have purchased in the last few months. Enter the name of a product in the search window, including the brand name like "iPod" or "Sony" or "Toyota." Press the Google Search button.

3. Scroll through and look at the AdWords ads listed for your products. Are there any that are relevant ads or that can provide you with relevant information about the product you purchased? List the three most relevant sponsored AdWords links.

Headline: _____

Display URL: _____

Headline: _____

Display URL: _____

Headline: _____

Display URL: _____

4. Explain which of the three AdWords headlines listed above caught your attention first and why.

5. Which of the three ads gives the most useful information about your product? Why?

Topic 5

AdWords Ads Appear Across Many Websites

Google **distributes** its search results and ads to a network of partners making up **Google's search and content network**. This means that advertisers can choose to display their ads across these partner sites—in addition to having them displayed on Google.com.

The Google Search Network

The Google search network is comprised of many products and search engines, such as America Online, CompuServe, Netscape, AT&T Worldnet, EarthLink, and others.

Image 1-9: Some of Google's search network partners.

The Google Content Network

Google's content network includes news pages, special-interest websites, and blogs. It includes large media sites like The New York Times as well as small publishers like BabyCenter.com. These sites partner with Google as part of the **AdSense** program (discussed in chapter 10). The Google content network gives advertisers a way to maximize their ad exposure by potentially appearing on millions of high-quality web pages.

Via **contextual placement**, Google checks the subject or theme of a specific website and places related ads on it. For example, Google might place ads for digital cameras on a website that reviews camera equipment.

AdWords' content network reaches 64% of individuals who use the Internet worldwide. These users speak more than 20 languages and live in over 100 countries. Together, Google's content network and Google's search network reaches four out of every five individuals online.

Image 1-10: Above are some of Google's content partners. These publishers participate in the AdWords program.

More: Mastering AdWords gives you a skill you can use in many companies. Some people choose a career as search engine marketers (SEMs). These individuals develop expertise in search advertising. For example, Google Advertising Professionals (GAP) are online marketing professionals with specialized expertise in managing AdWords accounts. Google Advertising Professionals must meet several requirements to get permission to use the GAP designation, such as passing an advanced AdWords exam.

An AdWords Success Story

Founded in 1981 (before the Internet), American Meadows has grown to become one of the largest and most respected suppliers of flower seed in North America. After seeing the benefits of doing business online, founder Ray Allen moved American Meadows from generating sales primarily via a print catalog to being a web-based business. In doing so, he faced three basic challenges of Internet advertising:

• Keeping ad copy current and compelling
• Monitoring site traffic
• Tracking clickthroughs and conversions (discussed in later lessons)

"With Google, I can target advertisements using very specific keywords and drive traffic to American Meadows," says Allen. "I can even reach customers looking for a particular wildflower species. This gives us a targeted advertising solution at a low cost and with a high return."

American Meadows typically receives more than 2,000 **unique visitors** per day. Since running its first Google AdWords campaign early in 2001, the company has increased leads by more than 120% per month.

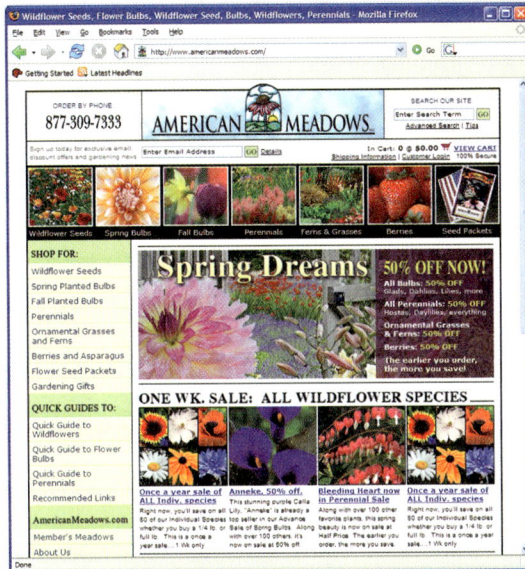

Image 1-11: American Meadows is a prominent flower seed supplier that uses AdWords.

Activity 1-3

Write responses to each of the following questions and statements:

a. What is the current state of online marketing and advertising? How has it improved since its earliest beginnings in the early 1990s?

b. Explain in your own words how search marketing works.

c. Explain the differences between organic and sponsored search results on Google.

d. Explain some of the possible advantages of online advertising versus traditional approaches. How can the addition of online advertising improve the marketing mix for certain products?

Key Takeaways

- Online advertising has experienced explosive growth due to technological advances and changing societal habits.

- The three R's (reach, relevance, and ROI) are important online advertising components.

- A search query begins when someone enters a keyword into the search bar. The organic (natural) results that appear are determined by Google's search algorithms and cannot be purchased as advertising.

- AdWords ads appear alongside and sometimes above Google search results pages. Ad display and placement are determined by relevancy of the keywords entered, price, and other factors.

- AdWords ads are made up of a headline, description, and display URL.

- AdWords ads can appear across the many search and content sites that are part of Google's network.

Vocabulary

- Ad copy
- AdSense
- AdWords
- Algorithms
- Cached
- Campaign
- Channel
- Contextual placement
- Display URL
- Distribution
- GAP
- Google Advertising Professional
- Google content network
- Google Network
- Google search button
- Google search network
- Headline
- Indexing

- Keyword
- Keyword targeted
- Marketing mix
- PageRank™
- Query
- Reach
- Relevance
- Return on Investment (ROI)
- Search Engine Marketing
- Search result
- Search results page
- SEM
- Similar Pages
- Sponsored Links
- Target
- Uniform Resource Locator (URL)
- Unique visitors
- Users

Google Advertising Professional Exam Preparation

To prepare for the Google Advertising Professional qualification exam, study the following lessons at the AdWords Learning Center, (**www.google.com/adwords/learningcenter**):

• Introduction to AdWords

Useful Links

The Google AdWords homepage, where you can sign up or log in.
Adwords.google.com

The Google AdWords Help Center, where you can find answers to questions.
Adwords.google.com/support

Google Technology.
www.google.com/technology/

Google's Advertising Programs: AdWords and AdSense.
www.google.com/ads

The Google Network and ad distribution site.
www.google.com/adwords/network

Quiz 1

1. The keywords a user types into Google's search engine to find information on the Internet are referred to as a search _____.

a. phrase
b. result
c. definition
d. query
e. engine

2. How many total lines are there in an AdWords text ad?

a. 2
b. 3
c. 4
d. 5
e. it varies

3. Which is not one of the three R's of advertising necessary for a successful ad campaign?

a. Reach
b. Rewards
c. Relevance
d. ROI

4. AdWords ads appear on Google's search results page under the heading _____.

a. Sponsored Ads
b. Sponsored Sites
c. AdWords Ads
d. Sponsored Links
e. Sponsored AdWords

5. The last line of ad text in an AdWords ad is called the _____.

a. Email address
b. Destination address
c. Display URL
d. Heading URL
e. Web address

6. Google accepts money for the placement of websites in organic search results

a. True
b. False

7. When you create a Google AdWords account, your ads will only be shown on Google's search results page.

a. True
b. False

Lesson 2

Overview of Google AdWords Accounts

Detailed Objectives:

At the end of this lesson, students should be able to:

- Set up an AdWords Starter Edition account
- Describe how AdWords accounts are structured
- Describe the auction system
- Explain how AdWords ads are ranked and priced
- Explain the key benefits of site targeting
- Describe the differences between keyword- and site-targeted campaigns
- Explain the available AdWords ad formats
- Explain how to choose sites for a site-targeted campaign

Getting Started: AdWords Starter Edition

The easiest way to start advertising on Google is to create an AdWords Starter Edition account. You can do this even if you don't have a website. Within a few minutes, Starter Edition enables any business operator to start showing ads, getting clicks and new customers.

Advertisers answer 8 simple questions to get started:

1) Where are your customers located?

2) What language will your ad be written in?

3) What website will your ad link to?

Users who click your ad will be sent to this website. If you don't have a website, you can create one in a few minutes.

4) What will your ad say?

You can write your own ad, or start with free ad ideas from Google.

5) Which keywords do you want to trigger your ad?

When people search Google for the keywords you choose here, your ad may appear alongside their search results. Keywords must be directly related to your ad.

6) What is your payment currency?

This is the currency in which you will be billed (usually US$).

7) What is your monthly budget?

AdWords shows your ad as often as possible within the budget you set. You're charged a small portion of the budget each time a user clicks your ad, so the higher your budget, the more ad impressions and clicks you may receive. You won't be charged more than this amount each month (though in some cases you may be charged less).

8) How do you want Google to contact you in the future?

Activity 2-1

Pick a business that you like that has a web page, and create an AdWords Starter Edition account for this business. Write down the information you enter.

1) Business name: _____

2) Open your Internet browser and navigate to adwords.google.com.

3) Click the 'Let's get started' button.

4) Select the Starter Edition option.

5) Enter the business's phone number if appropriate.

6) Click 'Continue.'

7) Enter a city name or postal code to target: _____

8) Click the language you want to target.

9) Type the site to which your ad will link:
   URL: _____

10) Write your ad:

    _____

    _____

    _____

11) Choose your keywords (20 or fewer):

    _____

    _____

    _____

12) Select a monthly budget. Explain why you chose this amount.

    _____

    _____

    _____

13) Select your future contact preferences.

14) Click 'Continue.' If you have permission to activate this account and provide billing information, do so. Otherwise click 'Cancel.'

AdWords Standard Edition

AdWords Standard Edition gives users a broad range of adverting features, far beyond what is available in Starter Edition. The rest of this text focuses on Standard Edition, but many of the principles apply to either edition.

Standard Edition Account Structure

An AdWords account is broken into three main levels. At the top level is **account**, then comes **campaign**, and then ad group.

- Accounts can hold multiple campaigns.
- Campaigns can hold multiple ad groups.
- Ad groups can contain multiple ads and keywords.

The basic idea behind the AdWords structure is versatility. AdWords gives advertisers many options – to run one ad on a few keywords, or hundreds of ads on thousands of keywords.

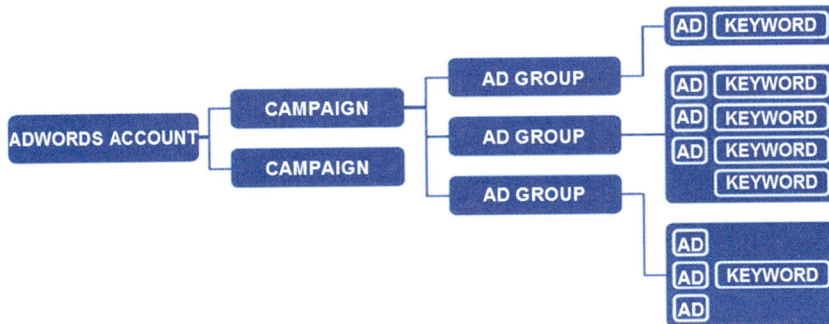

Image 2-1: The structure of an AdWords account.

Account

The account level contains campaigns. The account holder's email address and billing information are stored under the 'My Account' tab, shown in Image 2-2. These settings remain the same for everything throughout an AdWords account.

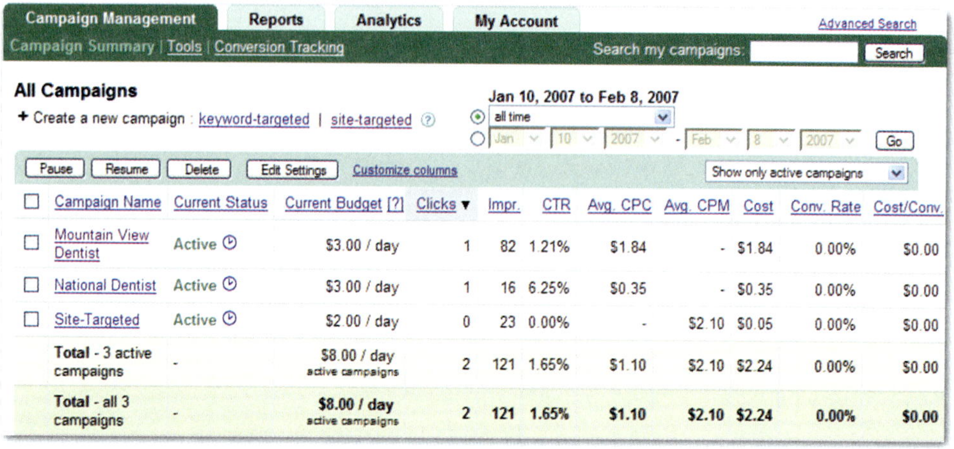

Image 2-2: The account level of the 'Campaign Management' tab of an AdWords account. Campaign names and related stats are shown at this level.

Campaign

There are two types of AdWords campaigns: **keyword-targeted** and **site-targeted**. Keyword-targeted campaigns (Google's standard and more popular type) let advertisers run ads on Google.com and across the entire Google Network. Site-targeted campaigns let advertisers choose individual sites in the Google content network where they'd like their ads to appear.

Keyword- and site-targeted campaigns share many attributes. The main differences are how the ads are targeted and the **pricing models**. Keyword targeting uses a **cost-per-click (CPC)** pricing model. Site targeting uses a **cost-per-thousand impressions (CPM)** pricing model, where an **impression** occurs each time an ad appears to a user. Unless explicitly stated otherwise, the material covered in this text focuses on keyword-targeted campaigns and ads.

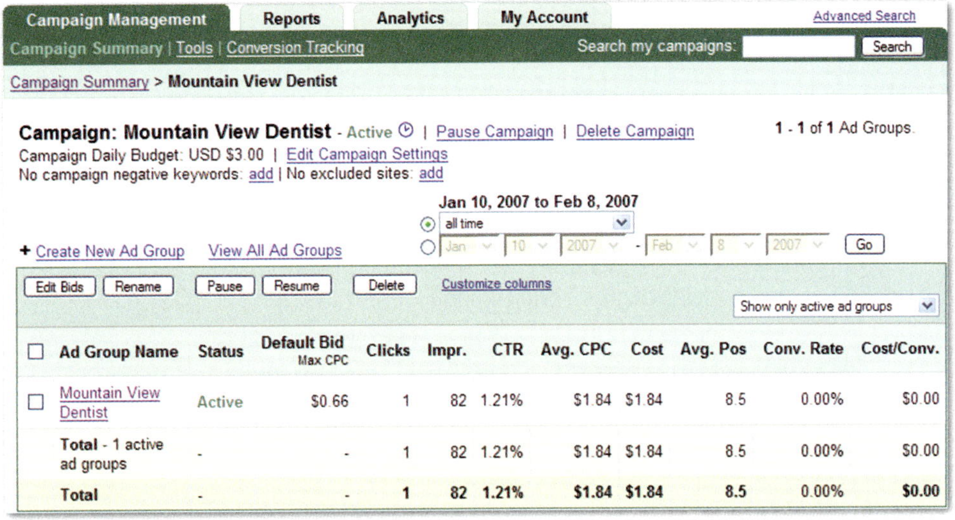

Image 2-3: The campaign level of a 'Campaign Management' tab of an AdWords account. Ad group names and related stats are shown at this level.

More: M is the Roman numeral for 1000 – hence CPM.

Each campaign (whether keyword- or site-targeted) has several settings independent of other campaigns. These settings include:

- Campaign name: the name of a campaign.

- End date: controls the campaign's duration. Unless end date is selected, Google ads run continuously by default.

- Daily budget: the amount of money an advertiser is willing to spend per day in a specific campaign. Google stops showing ads in a campaign when the daily budget is reached. Normal ad delivery starts again the next day.

- Distribution preferences: controls where the ad shows online. Options include the Google homepage, the search network, and the content network.

- Language targeting: targets the campaign to users who speak specific languages. When targeting a language like Spanish, Google only shows ads on Spanish-speaking Google domains (like www.google.es) or to searchers whose user preferences on google.com match that language.

- Location targeting: specifies geographic areas, like countries and cities, in which to show the ad. Customized location targeting gives advertisers two additional options:

- Target a circular area around an address.

- Target any shape defined by drawing lines on a map.

- Ad scheduling: defines which time of day ads run. Advanced mode can change bids automatically during different parts of the day.

- Position preference: aims to show ad in a specified position (for example, the top spot). Choosing a lower position will typically result in a lower CPC.

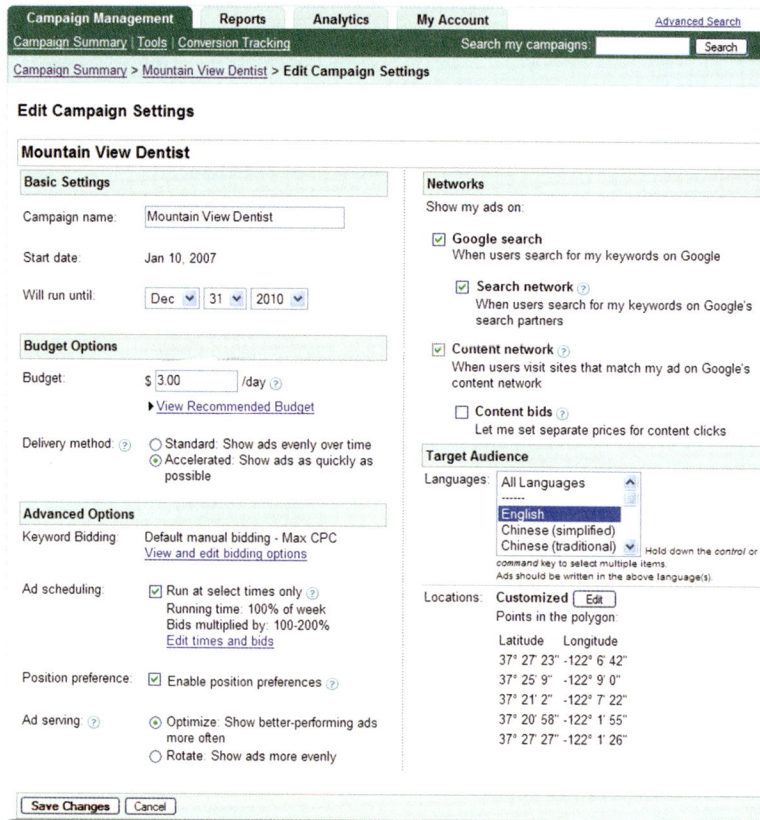

Image 2-4: An Edit Campaign Settings page in an AdWords account.

Ad Group

An ad group contains one or more ads and a set of related keywords. Ad groups work best when keywords and ad text focus on a single product or theme.

For example, one ad group might include keywords and ad text for coffee products (like "whole bean coffee"). Another ad group might contain keywords and ad text for tea products, and so on. When a user searches for the keyword "whole bean coffee", only the ad in the coffee ad group shows.

Another important component of the ad group (in a keyword-targeted campaign) is **maximum cost-per-click (Max CPC)**. This is the maximum amount an advertiser is willing to spend each time a user clicks the ad. An advertiser can choose one CPC for the entire ad group or select different CPCs for individual keywords.

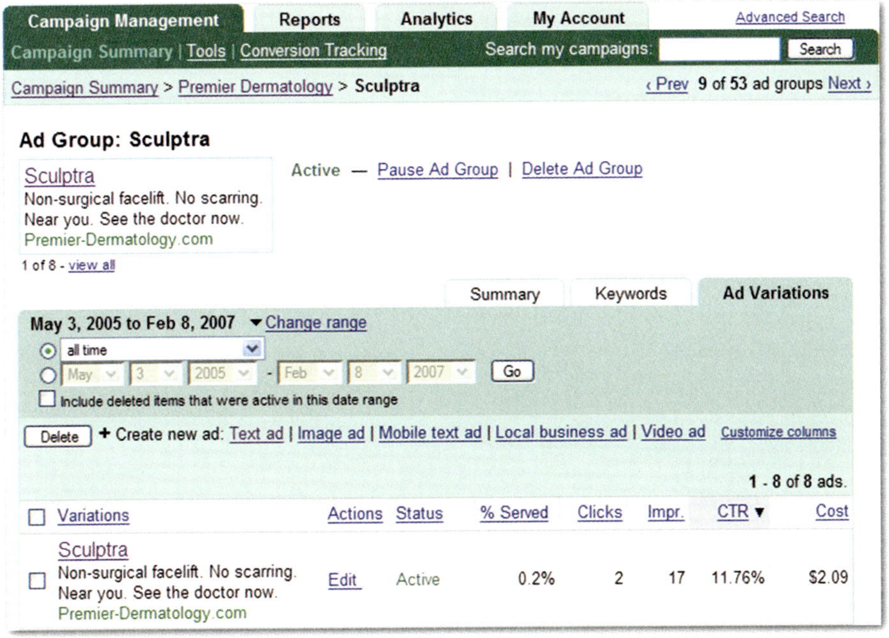

Image 2-5: The ad group level appears within the 'Campaign Management' tab of an AdWords account. Notice the three sub-tabs: 'Summary,' 'Keywords,' and 'Ad Variations.'

Activity 2-2

Set Up an AdWords Account

1. Open your web browser, and go to adwords.google.com.

2. Select the 'Sign Up Now' button.

3. Follow the steps to create an account. Create a list of questions you have.

4. Visit the 'Help' link located on the upper-right corner of the page to see if you can find the answers to the questions you wrote down in step 3.

5. Navigate to the account level view. Take a screenshot (Ctrl-Print Screen). Paste it in your write-up.

6. Navigate to the campaign level view. Take a screenshot.

7. Navigate to the campaign settings page. Take a screenshot.

8. Navigate to the ad group level. Take a screenshot.

9. Include all screenshots with your list of questions.

How Ads Are Shown: The AdWords Auction

AdWords runs an **auction** to help decide which ads to show. There are two basic ideas behind the auction: cost and quality. Well-designed ad campaigns have a perfect balance of the two. Since different advertisers might bid for the same keyword, Google has defined a way to determine which ad is most eligible and relevant to show. First, Google looks at cost. Google considers each advertiser's maximum CPC bid (Max CPC) for the keyword entered.

Then Google looks at relevance – that is, which ads match a user's search query as closely as possible. Google measures relevance through Quality Score, a numeric rating of the keyword's and related ad's quality. The Quality Score is based on several factors. These include:

• A keyword's click-through rate (CTR). This is the number of clicks an ad receives divided by the number of impressions.

• Ad text relevance (such as if the ad text contains a keyword).

• Overall historical keyword performance with Google (i.e. how the keyword has performed in the past).

• User experience on the landing page or site associated with an ad.

Google uses Quality Score to assign a minimum CPC bid for each keyword. This is the minimum amount an advertiser pays for an ad to run. If the keyword's Max CPC meets or exceeds the minimum CPC bid, the ad is eligible to enter the ad auction.

More: Terminology can get confusing. Keep in mind the different meanings between minimum CPC bid and maximum CPC bid. Here's a recap:

• Minimum CPC bid is the minimum amount an advertiser pays to run an ad. It's set by the AdWords system.

• Maximum CPC bid is the maximum amount an advertiser is willing to pay when someone clicks his ad. It's set by the advertiser.

AdWord's pricing system is designed to reward more relevant ads and keywords. Therefore, high Quality Scores drive down ad cost. A low Quality Score means the system has determined that an ad isn't very relevant to a keyword, and is therefore likely to perform poorly. The minimum CPC bid to run the ad goes up. On the other hand, a high Quality Score means the ad is very relevant to a keyword. The minimum CPC bid to run an ad drops.

Activity 2-3

How might you improve the Quality Score of the following keywords?

Ad	Keywords
Wedding Photographer Finest quality wedding photography. Make your album a rare treasure. JadeStudioProductions.com	wedding photographer find wedding photographer photographer for wedding wedding videographer videography for wedding videographer for wedding wedding videos

Why an auction?

AdWords has designed an auction system for fairness. In other advertising channels (such as newspapers), ad placement is based on cost. However, with AdWords, the key is quality advertising. Advertisers – big and small – can run keywords based on their marketing objectives. The auction pricing model sets a level playing field for all advertisers. The top spot can't necessarily be bought because the auction is constantly changing.

Ad Rank, AdWords Discounter, and Basic Tenets of Optimization

After a keyword enters the auction, the ad's rank determines the ad's actual position on a search results page. Keyword-targeted ads are ranked on search results pages based on their maximum CPC and Quality Score.

Ad Rank = Maximum CPC x Quality Score

Once an ad's rank has been calculated, the **AdWords Discounter** reduces the CPC the advertiser actually pays to be the minimum amount needed to stay ranked above the next-lowest-ranked advertiser. In this way, advertisers can avoid paying their full max CPC bid, even for the top spot.

While there's no way to secure top position on a search results page, Quality Score (and hence ad rank) can be improved through **optimization**. Optimization is the modification of an ad campaign to improve the quality and performance of an ad. For example, optimizations may include the following actions:

• Adding a few new keywords

• Adjusting maximum CPC bids

• Reorganizing ad groups

• Rewriting ads

• Changing targeting options

• Adjusting keyword matching types

• Choosing relevant destination URLs

Through optimization, an advertiser can help lower ad costs without losing the position on a search results page. Remember: the higher the Quality Score, the lower the minimum CPC bid and price an advertiser pays when someone clicks the ad.

To recap how the auction system works:

1. An advertiser enters the keyword "bean bag chair" into his AdWords account.

2. Google assigns the keyword and ad a Quality Score based on relevancy factors.

3. A user enters "bean bag chair" into the Google search bar.

4. Google checks whether the advertiser's keyword is eligible to enter the auction. (Is the keyword's max CPC higher than the minimum CPC set by Google?)

5. If the keyword is eligible to enter, Google ranks the advertiser's ad on Google based on the ad's maximum CPC bid and Quality Score.

More: I can't see my ad! There are several common reasons why you may be unable to see your ad. Use the Ads Diagnostic Tool and the Disapproved Ads Tool to quickly determine why you're not seeing your ad. Access these tools via the Tools link on the Campaign Management tab.

Topic 4

Introduction to Site-Targeted Campaigns

As discussed, keyword-targeted ads can appear on Google search results pages or on search and content sites within the Google Network. Site-targeted campaigns, however, appear only on selected sites within the content network. Site targeting gives advertisers the ability to:

• Advertise on a favorite site or sites.

• Reach customers early in the buying process, with ads designed to increase awareness or to promote a brand, but not necessarily to generate clicks or traffic. This process is called **branding**.

Site-targeted campaigns are priced using a CPM model: The advertiser sets the maximum price he's willing to pay for every thousand impressions his ad gets on that site (called the **maximum CPM**). CPM ads accrue charges whenever the ad is shown, whether a user clicks the ad or not.

Keyword-Targeted Campaigns vs. Site-Targeted Campaigns

	Keyword-Targeted Campaign	Site-Targeted Campaign
How does the advertiser target customers?	By keywords.	By websites.
Where can ads appear?	On Google.com, on Google search partner sites, and on all content sites in the Google Network.	On individual sites the advertiser selects in the Google Network.
When can ads appear?	Whenever users search for keywords the advertiser has chosen. They may also appear, if selected, when users visit any Google Network site with content matching the keywords.	Whenever users visit the individual sites the advertiser selects from the Google Network.
How are ads priced?	Cost per click (CPC). The advertiser sets the price he'd like to pay each time a user clicks his ad. Google charges advertisers only when a user clicks their ad.	Cost per thousand impressions (CPM). The advertiser sets the price he'd like to pay for each 1,000 impressions the ad receives. Clicks don't matter – Google charges the advertiser whenever the ad is shown to a user.
What types of ads are supported?	Text ads, **expanded text ads**, and **image ads**.	Expanded text ads and image ads.

Creating a Site-Targeted Campaign

To create a site-targeted campaign, AdWords generates a list of potential content network sites on which to place an ad. Then the advertiser picks sites from the list. For AdWords to generate a list of sites to pick from, the advertiser must either:

- List URLs of sites where she would like to advertise (or that are similar to those on which she'd like to advertise). She can enter domains (like baseball-fever.com) or specific site sections (like baseball-fever.com/calendar).

- Describe topics that match her ads. For instance: soccer shoes.

- Select categories like Entertainment, and subcategories like Movies or Music.

- Select demographics of the target audience. Demographics include gender, age, income, and presence of children in household (Image 2-6).

Look for sites popular with these types of people.

Gender:	☑ female	☐ male			

Age:	✓	✓	✓	✓	✓	✓
	18-24	25-34	35-44	45-54	55-64	65+

Annual Household Income (USD):	✕	✕	✕	✕	✕	✓	✓
	0- 14,999	15,000-24,999	25,000-39,999	40,000-59,999	60,000-74,999	75,000-99,999	100,000+

▼ Advanced Options

Ethnicity: ⦿ Any
○ White/Caucasian
○ Black/African American
○ Asian/Pacific Islander
○ Hispanic

Children: ☑ children in household   ☑ no children in household

Note: Demographic data is currently available only for the United States.
Demographic data source: comScore Media Metrix, Total U.S. 2006/10

Reset all | Get Available Sites

Image 2-6: Here, an advertiser has used the site-selection tool to find sites whose audience is primarily women who make more than $75,000 per year.

More: The AdWords site-exclusion tool allows advertisers to select sites where they don't want their ads to appear.

More: Site targeting and animated-image ads are a great combination for branding.

Activity 2-4

Below are two fictional companies and their products and goals. Decide which type of campaign would be best for each (keyword-targeted or site-targeted), and explain your reasoning.

a. Video Palace offers DVD rentals online. DVDs are sent to the customer. The company's goal is to drive traffic to its site and increase its online sales. What type of AdWords campaign(s) would you select for Video Palace? Why?

b. Bertlesman & Love is an expanding clothing chain with locations in malls all over the United States. The company has a website that allows users to see new fashions and buy clothes, but the majority of its sales come from stores. B&L is a fairly new company and wants to promote its name to teens and twenty-somethings. What type of AdWords campaign(s) would you select for Bertlesman & Love? Why?

Site-Targeting Case Study: Paramount's Hustle and Flow

In 2005, Paramount wanted to promote its new film, Hustle and Flow. To market the film to the right audience, Paramount created a site-targeted ad campaign. Company representatives chose keywords that were relevant to the film, and AdWords generated a few hundred potential sites that matched. After selecting several sites from the list, Paramount observed the following in its exit polls:

• Thirty-five percent of opening weekend moviegoers said that the Internet was a key factor in their decision to see Hustle and Flow.

• An estimated 3 million unique users were exposed to the ads for this movie. Site targeting enabled Paramount to advertise to a specific and relevant audience.

(Source: Business Week Online, "Grabbing the Grassroots," 11/21/05).

Ranking Site-Targeted Ads

Site-targeted campaigns follow an auction system, similar to keyword-targeted campaigns. They compete with other CPM ads and with keyword-targeted CPC ads.

As with keyword advertising, the AdWords Discounter automatically reduces any winning CPM bid to the minimum necessary to keep the ad's position on the page (above its competition). As a result, the max CPM an advertiser sets is rarely the amount actually paid.

Some CPM ads may occupy the entire ad space on a webpage with an image ad, video ad, or an expanded text ad. In order for one of these ads to show, it has to outrank the total combined rank of the competing ads.

More: An expanded text ad fills an entire ad space on a content page on its own, rather than being grouped with other text ads. These ads look the same as regular text ads, but the text is enlarged. Any AdWords text ad can run as an expanded text ad. An ad is expanded automatically whenever the system determines that it is a good candidate to take the entire space.

Google site-targeted ads must maintain a very high level of relevancy, since they compete with keyword-targeted ads. If the keyword-targeted ads prove to be more relevant, the CPM ads are squeezed out. In addition, a minimum CPM is set to ensure that advertisers choose their ads and audiences with care.

Content Bids: Choosing Different Pricing Models by Campaign

So far, we've discussed an advertiser's ability to run a keyword-targeted campaign, a site-targeted campaign, or both. Some advertisers may find one or the other type of campaign more valuable. So AdWords allows advertisers to set different bid amounts on the content network through **content bids**.

Content bids allow the advertiser to set one price when their ads run on search sites and a separate price when their ads run on content sites. Content bids are usually a good option for businesses that receive greater success on content sites than on search sites (or vice versa).

Activity 2-5

1. Find a website in the Google content network (like about.com) and view the AdWords ads on that site. (They're labeled "Ads by Google" or "Sponsored Links.")

2. List the site that you visited.

3. Describe the story/content on the site.

4. Describe the most relevant ad on the site.

5. How well do the ads match the content on the site? Describe.

Ad Formats

Including text ads, AdWords offers five ways (called **ad formats**) in which advertisers can display their ads:

- **Text ad:** The most common AdWords format, text ads contain a 25-character title; 70-character, two-line description; and 35-character display URL. Text ads can appear across all sites in the Google Network.

- **Local business ad:** These ads are associated with a specific geographical location and are shown on Google Maps with an enhanced map component.

- **Mobile ad:** Mobile ads are short, text-based ads that appear when users search Google from a mobile device.

- **Image ad:** These are graphic ads, including drawings, photos, or animations, that appear on some content network sites.

- **Video ad:** Video ads are displayed as an unmoving image when the page loads. Once the user clicks the 'play' button, video begins playing within the ad space.

Image 2-7: Some of the AdWords ad formats.

Activity 2-6

Search the web for an online business. Make an advertising plan for the business.

1. Which location and which language would you target?

a. Location

   Countries: _____
   Regions: _____
   Customized: _____

b. Language: _____

c. Explain your choices.

2. Which ad formats would be best to use and why?

a. Ad format(s): _____

b. Explain your choices.

3. Where would you choose to distribute the ad or ads?

a. Google Search: _____

b. Search Network: ____ ____

c. Content Network: _____

d. Explain your choices.

Activity 2-7

Write up your responses to the following.

- Explain how an AdWords account is structured
- Explain CPM bidding
- Explain ad rank
- Explain how the Ad Discounter works
- List the AdWords ad formats

Key Takeaways

- An AdWords account structure is broken down into three levels: account, campaign, and ad group. Accounts can contain multiple campaigns. Campaigns can contain multiple ad groups. Ad Groups can hold multiple ads and keywords.

- There are two types of campaigns: keyword-targeted and site-targeted campaigns. These types of campaigns are similar in many ways, except for pricing and ad distribution options.

- Ad groups work best when organized into similarly themed keywords and ad text.

- AdWords operates an auction-based advertising environment. Keyword bids must meet the minimum CPC, determined by the Quality Score, to enter the AdWords auction.

- Keyword-targeted ads are ranked based on their maximum CPC and their Quality Score. An ad's rank decides its position on a search results page.

- The AdWords Discounter ensures an advertiser only pays the minimum amount to maintain a position above his competitor.

- Optimization helps improve Quality Score and reduce costs.

- A cost-per-thousand-impressions (CPM) pricing model is used with site-targeted campaigns. Advertisers are charged when their ad is shown.

- CPM ads are ranked based on max CPM. They can compete with other CPM or CPC ads.

- Site-targeted campaigns only appear on selected content sites in the AdWords content network. They're based on a CPM pricing model.

- Site targeting allows advertisers to choose sites in the Google content network where they would like their ad to show.

- Sites can be found by listing URLs, describing topics, browsing categories, and/or selecting audiences based on demographics.

- Content bids allow advertisers to set different prices for ads that appear on the content network and on the search network.

- AdWords offers five ad formats: text, local business, mobile, image, and video ads.

Vocabulary

- Account
- Ad formats
- Ad group
- Ad scheduling
- AdWords Discounter
- Animated ad
- Auction
- Brand
- Brand awareness
- Branding
- Campaign name
- Click-through rate
- Content bids
- Cost per click
- Cost per thousand impressions
- CPC
- CPM
- CTR
- Customized location-targeting
- Daily budget
- Distribution preferences
- Domains
- End date
- Expanded text ad
- Image ad
- Impression
- Language targeting
- Local business ad
- Location targeting
- Max CPC
- Maximum cost-per-click
- Maximum CPM
- Minimum CPC bid
- Mobile ad
- Position prcference
- Pricing model
- Quality Score
- Rank
- Site exclusion tool
- Site sections
- Site targeted
- User preferences (on google.com)
- Video ad

Google Advertising Professional Exam Preparation

To prepare for the Google Advertising Professional qualification examination, study the following lessons at the AdWords Learning Center (**www.google.com/adwords/learningcenter**):

- Account Types, Setup, and Structure
- Account Navigation
- Starting Off Right: Organization, Keywords, Ad Text
- Search and Contextual Targeting
- Site Targeting
- Language and Location Targeting
- Keyword Targeting

Helpful Links

The AdWords Help Discussion Group allows you to learn from other AdWords advertisers as they post their questions, answers, and tips about Google AdWords.

groups.google.com/group/adwords-help/topics

Quiz

1. What is the structure of an AdWords account from the top down?

a. Account> ad groups> campaigns> keywords and ad text
b. Account> budget> ad groups> keywords and campaigns
c. Account> ad groups> ad text> CPCs and keywords
d. Account> campaigns> ad groups> ad text and keywords
e. Account> keywords> ad text> CPCs and budgets

2. You can associate each campaign in an account with a unique budget, geographic target, and email contact preference.

a. True
b. False

3. You sell novels written in Spanish, and you ship worldwide. What would be the best targeting preference for your ad?

a. Target ads to the Spanish language, and to many Spanish-speaking countries around the world
b. Target ads to all languages, but restrict targeting to European countries
c. Target ads to the Spanish language, and to the countries of Mexico and Spain only

4. You will always be charged the maximum CPC you set for a keyword or ad group.

a. True
b. False

5. What is the fastest way to move up your ad's position on the page?

a. Optimize AdWords campaign for stronger CTR
b. Increase daily budget
c. Increase maximum cost-per-click (CPC)
d. Add location targets
e. Change keyword matching options

6. Google's contextual targeting automatically displays ads next to relevant content.

a. True
b. False

7. An AdWords ad accrued clicks on Blogger.com, Forbes.com, and Looksmart.com. These clicks came from _____.

a. Image ads
b. AdWords ads in email products and services
c. The Google network of search partners
d. The Google network of content sites

8. Site-targeted campaigns allow you to show ads on the:

a. Google search network
b. Google.com
c. Google content network
d. Google content network and Google.com

9. Which ad formats are acceptable for site-targeted campaigns?

a. text ads
b. image ads
c. video ads
d. pop-up ads

10. Demographic targeting allows advertisers to target audiences based on:

a. gender, age, and occupation
b. gender, age, and annual household income
c. gender, occupation, and family size
d. age, education, and annual household income

11. Site-targeted ads share the ad unit on a content page with how many other ads?

a. 3
b. between 7 and 9
c. 0
d. 2

12. Advertisers who want to increase brand awareness would benefit more from a traditional keyword campaign.

a. True
b. False

13. Your max CPM bid is _____.

a. the amount you are willing to pay for 1000 impressions
b. the amount you are willing to pay for 1000 clicks
c. the amount you are willing to pay for each impression
d. the amount you are willing to pay for the entire campaign

14. With CPM pricing, you are charged _____.

a. a flat rate per month
b. when your ad appears on a content page
c. when a user clicks on your ad

15. Site-targeted campaigns compete in a different auction than keyword campaigns.

a. True
b. False

Successful Keyword-Targeted Advertising

Detailed Objectives:

At the end of this lesson, students should be able to:

- Choose relevant keywords

- Define keyword-matching types

- Write compelling ad text

- Select landing pages

- Explain how keyword status, minimum cost-per-click (CPC) bid, and click-through rate (CTR) affect Quality Score

- Boost Quality Score through optimization

Choosing the Right Keywords

Selecting keywords is one of the most important parts of creating a successful AdWords campaign. To pick the best keywords, use this five-step process:

1) expand

2) match

3) scrub

4) group

5) refine

Step 1: Expand

First, come up with as many relevant keywords as possible. What does the business sell? What are the advertiser's goals? If it's to sell purebred puppies, some good keywords might be 'purebred puppies' and 'purebred dogs.' Even better are keywords focused on specific breeds, like "poodle." List all keywords that come to mind. It's a good idea to avoid less specific keywords, like 'dogs,' which usually cost more and usually don't relate to a user's specific search.

AdWords also provides a Keyword Tool (**www.google.com/adwords/keywordtool**) that generates keyword ideas (shown in Image 3-1). Access the Keyword Tool, enter keywords similar to the ones you want to find, and sort the results.

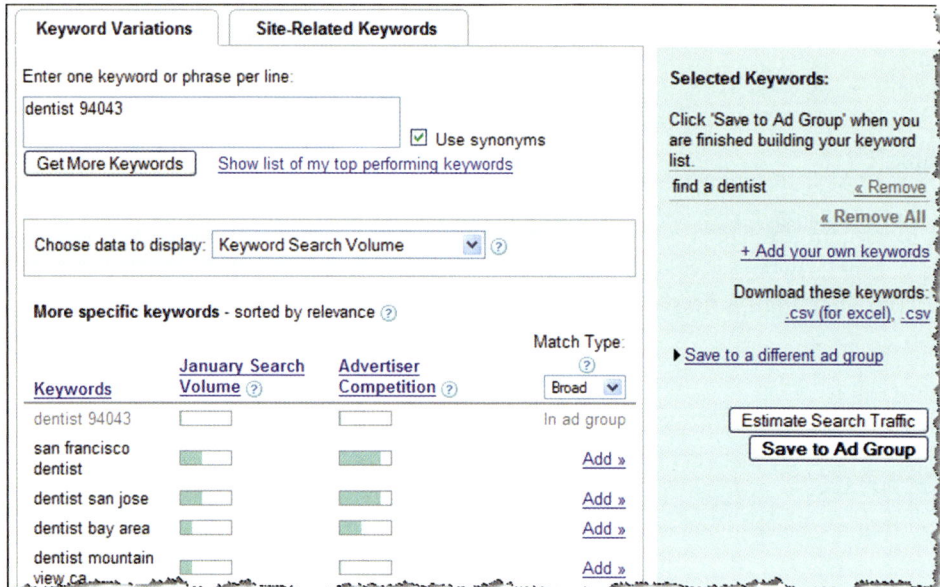

Image 3-1: The Google AdWords Keyword Tool

Step 2: Match

Google offers different **keyword-match types** to relate to a user's search. They include broad match, phrase match, exact match, and negative match.

- **Broad match** means that all searches using that word (in any order or combination) will display the ad. For example, 'purebred puppy' will show an ad for all searches with the words 'purebred' and 'puppy'. This could include searches for 'buy purebred puppy' and 'puppy that is purebred.' This is the default setting for all keywords.

- **Phrase match** requires the words to appear in order. "Purebred puppy" (entered with quotation marks) shows ads for searches with 'purebred' and 'puppy' in that order, as in 'purebred puppy Chihuahua.' Ads won't appear, however, for searches with any words between 'purebred' and 'puppy'. This narrows the audience.

- **Exact match** shows ads when the exact phrase is used in the search – without any other words before, between, or after. So '[purebred puppy]' (with brackets) shows an ad for searches with just the words 'purebred puppy', not 'purebred puppy advice' or 'purebred puppy veterinarian.' This further narrows the audience.

- **Negative match** eliminates phrases for which an advertiser doesn't want an ad to appear, such as 'cheap' or 'free'. Negative matches are selected by entering negative keywords with a minus sign, such as '-free.' This option prevents an ad from showing to people searching for 'free purebred puppy.'

Step 3: Scrub

AdWords is geared toward relevance. Keywords that maintain the same standard give strong results. Irrelevant keywords should be removed from the keyword list. Delete any words that don't relate to the advertiser's business. Two- to three-word phrases are usually best.

Step 4: Group

Keywords should be organized into similar themes, products, or types in separate ad groups. This way, each ad can be written specifically for similarly grouped keywords.

For example, here's a good way to separate keywords for chocolates into three different ad groups:

Boxed Chocolate	Valentine's Chocolates	Swiss Chocolate
Keywords: • boxed chocolate • chocolate gifts • assorted boxed chocolates • gourmet chocolates	Keywords: • valentine chocolates • valentines chocolates • buy valentines chocolates • valentines candy • valentines chocolate box	Keywords: • swiss milk chocolate • swiss dark chocolate • swiss chocolate

Step 5: Test and Refine

Users are constantly searching for different things, so advertisers must regularly test and refine keywords. Build on keywords that work, and delete others that don't.

Writing Successful Ad Text

Writing ads is an art. The best way to see which ads bring the best results is to write three or four at one time. Then, let them gather at least 1,000 impressions. Ads with the highest CTR are top performers. Below are some tips to help create compelling ad text.

- Text should be clear and well-written. It should highlight the **differentiating characteristics** of an advertiser's product or service.

- Include keywords in the ad title. Since the keyword entered is what people are looking for, ads with keywords in the title stand out. Also, keywords that a user enters into Google.com appear in bold in the ad.

- Include prices and promotions. Users tend to click on ads that give more information about the advertiser's product.

- Include a **call to action**. Calls to action are generally action verbs, such as buy, order, and purchase. While find and search may be accurate, these words imply that the user is still in awareness/interest mode. Generic actions like *click here* are discouraged.

- Avoid using a company name or website domain in the ad text. This technique doesn't typically attract more clicks unless advertising for an established company with a compelling brand.

- Capitalize the words in the display URL. For example, instead of using www.warmpuppies.com, use WarmPuppies.com.

- Choose a destination URL that points the visitor to a **landing page** relevant to the keyword entered. Users who don't find what is promised immediately are more likely to leave the advertiser's site. Promotions and particular products mentioned in the ad should be visible on the landing page.

Activity 3-1

1. Visit Google.com and perform a search for any product that you'd like to buy.

2. Find an AdWords ad that you think is well written.

3. Explain why you think this ad is successful.

4. For the same search results, find an ad that you think is written less well.

5. Explain why.

6. Re-write the second ad copy.

Activity 3-2: What's wrong with this ad?

Name all the problems – relevancy and guideline issues – that you see with this ad:

Just What You Want
Frothing Latte Bean has many
different types of coffee you luv!
www.frothing-latte-bean.com

Choosing Relevant Landing Pages

The landing page is the place where a user "lands" after clicking an advertiser's ad. Advertisers who point users to high-quality, relevant landing pages build trust with a potential customer.

AdWords measures landing page quality. Landing pages with useful, informative content in relation to an advertiser's keywords and ad text receive higher Quality Scores. In general, the landing page should:

• Allow users to easily find what the ad promises

• Openly share information about the business

• Clearly define what the business is or offers

Here are three tips to help give users a high-quality experience and build trust. An advertiser should:

1. Provide relevant and substantial content:

  • Landing pages should provide useful and accurate information about the product or service in the ad

  • Unique page content and layout help users differentiate one site from others

2. Treat a user's personal information responsibly. Sites should:

  • Provide as much access as possible to the site without requiring users to register

  • Provide facts on how any personal information is gathered

  • Explain how the advertiser uses, or will potentially use, personal information

  • Give users options to limit the use of their personal information

3. Develop a site that's easy to navigate. The key to turning visitors into customers is making it easy for them to find what they want. Therefore, a website should guide users from the landing page, through the transaction, to checkout. Websites should:

  • Provide an easy path for users to purchase a product in the ad

  • Avoid obtrusive elements like pop-ups

Activity 3-3

1. Visit a website where you've purchased something in the past.

2. List the name.

3. Navigate through the site by clicking on links and searching for products. Critique how easy or difficult it is to navigate through the site by answering the following questions:

- What are the strengths of this website?

- What are the weaknesses?

- If you were the webmaster of this site, how would you improve it to provide a better user experience?

4. Select a landing page and write an AdWords ad that fits the content of that page.

Monitoring Performance and Analyzing an Ad's Quality Score

An advertiser enters a keyword and ad into the system. Now what? With traditional advertising, the work is done. However, with online advertising, monitoring performance and maintenance are part of the advertising model. Most importantly, advertisers should pay attention to Quality Score.

Recall that Quality Score measures an ad's relevance and sets the minimum CPC bid required for an ad to enter the auction. Ads with higher Quality Scores tend to:

- get more clicks
- be shown in higher positions on search results pages
- bring more businesses and customers together

Keyword Status

Keyword status determines whether an ad is eligible to run in the auction. In other words, it determines whether a keyword is eligible to trigger ads on search pages. The keyword status appears in the ad group view (Image 3-2). There are two keyword statuses:

- **Active:** The keyword is eligible to run in the auction (the maximum CPC bid is above the minimum CPC bid required)
- **Inactive for search:** The keyword isn't eligible to run on Google or on Google's search network because the maximum CPC bid is below the minimum CPC required. (Note that the ad may still be shown on the content network.)

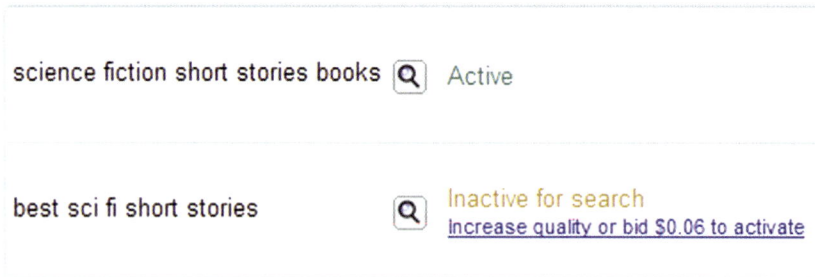

science fiction short stories books [Q]	Active
best sci fi short stories [Q]	Inactive for search Increase quality or bid $0.06 to activate

Image 3-2: Keywords can have two statuses: active and inactive for search.

If keywords are inactive for search, the system offers a minimum bid required to activate that keyword. There are four ways to reactivate an inactive-for-search keyword:

1. Increase the keyword's Quality Score through optimization.

2. Increase the keyword's maximum CPC bid to the minimum bid suggested by the AdWords system.

3. Delete the keyword (if the minimum CPC bid to reactivate it is too expensive).

4. Do nothing. Occasionally, as AdWords gathers more data about a keyword (or as the factors incorporated in Quality Score change) a keyword may be re-activated without any action from the advertiser. However, doing nothing is not recommended.

Topic 5

How Do Advertisers Know Their Quality Score?

For advertisers, the minimum CPC bid is the best overall gauge of Quality Score. This is because they're inversely related – the less relevant the keyword, the higher the minimum CPC bid, and vice versa.

For example, a keyword that performs well over time will have an increased Quality Score and a decreased minimum CPC bid. Also, recall that the AdWords Discounter automatically reduces the actual CPC paid, so an advertiser pays the lowest price possible to maintain an ad's position on the page. This means that the higher the Quality Score, the lower the cost when someone clicks an ad.

The best way to maintain a high-quality, cost-effective campaign is to keep close tabs on account **metrics**. Metrics appear in an advertiser's account for each campaign, each ad group, and each keyword. Pay special attention to metrics for keyword status, minimum CPC bid, and CTR. Well-run campaigns have:

• 'Active' keyword statuses

• Low minimum CPC bids

• High CTRs

If a campaign doesn't have one or several of the above components, it can be improved through optimization.

Status ▼ ⑦	Current Bid Max CPC	Clicks	Impr.	CTR	Avg. CPC	Cost	Avg. Pos
Active	$0.33	2	35	5.71%	$0.04	$0.07	1.6

Image 3-3: Some of the metrics available in an account.

Topic 6

Optimize Ads to Boost Performance and Quality Score

So far this lesson has covered strategies for developing effective keyword lists, writing quality ad text, and choosing relevant landing pages. Low Quality Scores usually stem from a problem in one of these areas.

Therefore, an advertiser can boost performance and Quality Score by picking and refining relevant keywords, writing powerful ad text, creating high-quality landing pages, and constantly testing and monitoring which techniques work best.

In summary, here are some optimization tricks to boost performance:

• Use two- to three-word keyword phrases

• Use keyword matching options

• Make sure keywords relate to the product

• Use keyword variations (such as synonyms or alternate spellings)

• Create similar keyword groupings, or themes, in each ad group, and ads that focus on that group

• Write clear, compelling ad text

• Include keywords in the ad text and title

• Include a call to action in the ad text

• Send users to the best possible landing page

• Test multiple ads per ad group

Key Takeaways

- Choosing the best keywords involves a five-step process. Keywords should relate to site content, be at least two words long, and be specific.

- Advertisers can target their keywords by match type: broad match, phrase match, exact match, and negative match.

- The Keyword Tool and Traffic Estimator assist advertisers in selecting keywords.

- Ad text should be clear, compelling, and accurate. Include keywords in the headline or ad text.

- The landing page should reflect the advertiser's ad text. It should be easy to navigate and it should provide relevant and substantial content.

- Quality Score affects the status of keywords (active or inactive for search) and determines whether an ad is eligible to compete in the ad auction.

- Minimum CPC bid is the best gauge of a keyword's Quality Score. They have an inverse relationship.

- Account performance metrics (such as CTR and minimum CPC bid) are good indicators of an ad's Quality Score.

- Optimization involves monitoring account metrics and continuing to refine and test ad copy, keywords, and landing pages to see what works.

Vocabulary

- Keyword match types
- Broad match
- Phrase match keywords
- Exact match keywords
- Negative match keywords
- Differentiating characteristics
- Call to action
- Keyword's status
- 'Inactive for Search'
- Metrics
- Navigate
- Optimization

Google Advertising Professional Exam Preparation

If you wish to prepare for the Google Advertising Professional qualification examination, study the following lessons at the AdWords Learning Center (**www.google.com/adwords/learningcenter**):

• Optimization Overview

• Your Website

• Your Account

• Specific Optimization Strategies

Useful Links

Landing Page and Site Quality Guidelines:
https://adwords.google.com/support/bin/answer.py?answer=47884

Google AdWords Editorial Guidelines to help you create effective ads:
adwords.google.com/select/guidelines.html

Webmaster Guidelines for recommendations to help your site perform better in Google's search results and improve the quality of your landing pages:
www.google.com/support/webmasters/bin/answer.py?answer=35769

Quiz

1. Quality Score is determined by _____.

a. Max CPC
b. Keyword click-through rate, ad text relevance, historical keyword performance, and other relevancy factors
c. Max CPC and click-through rate
d. Daily budget

2. _____ ensures a positive user experience, and keeps users returning to Google.

a. Low CPC
b. Promotional ad text
c. Recognition
d. Relevance

3. Which two of the following are keyword states? (Select 2)

a. Active
b. Inactive for search
c. Discontinued
d. Abnormal

4. Keywords that are "Active" _____.

a. have a Max CPC lower than the minimum CPC bid
b. show ads with limited delivery
c. have a poor Quality Score
d. have a Max CPC at or above the minimum CPC bid

5. Which three of the following are characteristics of effective landing pages? (Select 3)

a. Easy to navigate
b. Text-only
c. Display product specified by keyword
d. Relevant to the ad text

6. Which of the following would be a good landing page for the keyword 'Valentine's dark chocolate'?

a. A page within the site selling dark and white chocolates only
b. The site's homepage
c. A page within the site selling dark chocolates in a heart-shaped box
d. A page within the site selling the best deal on cheap Christmas chocolates

7. The purpose of the Keyword Tool is _____.

a. to determine the Quality Score of the keywords in your account
b. to generate possible keyword variations
c. to analyze the relevancy of your chosen keywords
d. to count the number of keywords each Ad Group contains

8. Ad groups with specific keywords targeted to specific products tend to have _____ conversion rates with _____ ad impressions.

a. lower, more
b. higher, fewer
c. higher, more
d. lower, fewer

Image and Video Ads

Detailed Objectives

At the end of this lesson, students should be able to:

- Explain how image and video ads differ from text ads
- Describe different formats for image ads and video ads
- Explain advantages of using video and image ads
- Create successful image and video advertising plans

Overview of Image Ads

AdWords **image ads** are graphic ads that can be still (motionless) or **animated**. These ads appear on select sites in the Google content network (not search sites) which have opted in to the image ads program. Image ads combine two features – graphics and AdWords targeting technology. This gives advertisers the power of pictures along with the precision of matching ads to related content sites.

Still image ads can be formatted in .gif, .jpg, and .png. Animated image ads can be formatted in .gif or Flash. Both types can be in the following sizes (in **pixels**):

- 250 x 250 Square
- 200 x 200 Small Square
- 468 x 60 Banner
- 728 x 90 Leaderboard
- 300 x 250 Inline Rectangle
- 336 x 280 Large Rectangle
- 120 x 600 Skyscraper
- 160 x 600 Wide Skyscraper

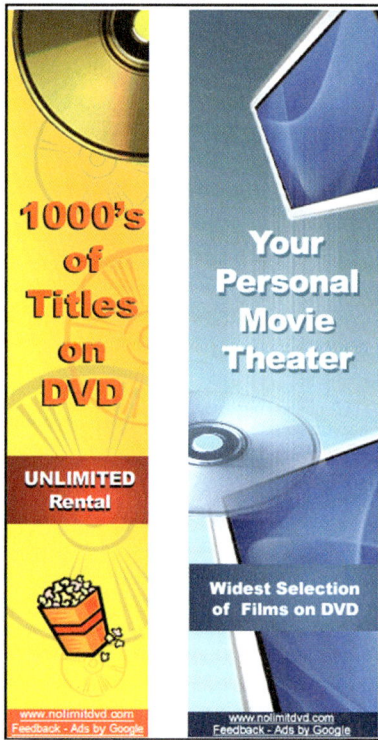

Image 4-1: Some examples of AdWords image ads.

Google image ads display the destination URL so users know where they'll end up after clicking the ad (as seen in Image 4-2).

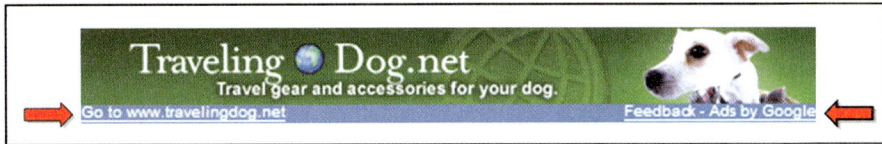

Image 4-2: Image ads contain a display URL.

Activity 4-1

1. Find a site you like that publishes image ads.

2. Critique an image ad:

a. Describe the ad. Is this ad visually appealing? Is it still or animated? Does it catch your eye? Why?

b. Do you think the ad is effective or compelling for its target audience?

c. Which format does the ad use? Is it a banner? Leaderboard?

d. Explain why you think the advertiser chose to create an image ad as opposed to a text ad.

Activity 4-2

Create an image ad of your own. Don't worry about your artistic skills.

1. Start by selecting a small business or any product you wish to advertise. Clear your selection with your instructor.

2. Create a **mock-up** of your ad, on paper if you wish, sketching out the graphics and the text that will appear on the image ad.

3. If you have the proper software and skills, create your image ad (optional).

Video Ads

Video ads are **click-to-play** ads that appear on both content and search sites in the Google Network. They appear as a static (not moving) **opening image**, and users must click the 'play' button or the opening image to watch the video. If a user clicks the display URL at the bottom of the ad or clicks the ad while it's playing, the user goes to the advertiser's website.

When paying on a CPC basis (keyword targeted), advertisers pay for clickthroughs leading users to their website, not for clicks on the opening image or 'play' button. When paying on a CPM basis (site targeted), advertisers pay for impressions of the opening image, rather than plays of the video.

Video ads let users interact with an ad. For example, users can control the volume and replay the video. This increases the level of engagement users have with an ad (as opposed to TV, where users watch ads passively).

Image 4-3: Click-to-play: Video ads allow users to click on these ads in order to watch the video.

Google **hosts** and **streams video feeds**. Streaming technology is optimized for all bandwidths (dial-up, DSL, etc.).The video operates as a **Flash** element. Flash is software for creating animated graphics and video. Most browsers have the capability to play Flash. As a result, users don't have to install anything to play a video. As a website publisher, it is important to consider the placement of a video ad on a web page. If there is other important content on the page, for instance, the video ad may be better placed within a column of text so people are encouraged to read something before they click and view the video.

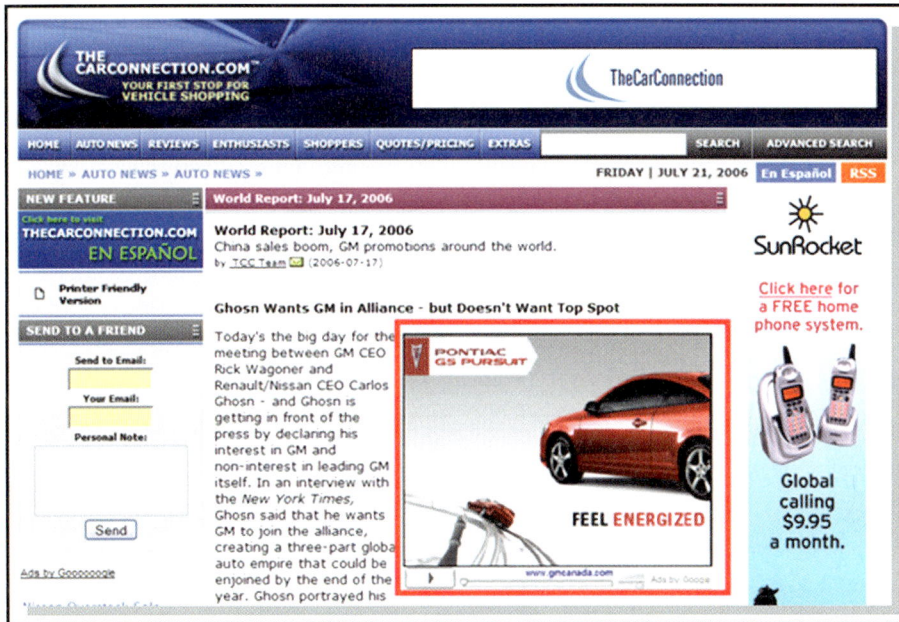

Image 4-4: Publishers place video ads strategically on web pages for maximum impact.

More: Keep it fresh: Advertisers must monitor play rates carefully. If an ad's play rate starts falling off, repeat visitors to the web page serving the ad have probably already viewed the video and aren't replaying it. This would be a good signal that new video ads are needed to keep potential customers interested.

Tips on Creating Successful Video Ads

When creating a video ad, follow these tips:

- Create a descriptive and eye-catching opening image (the image which users see before playing the video).

- Entice users to click 'play' by using rich, sharp colors.

- Include a few words to describe the product, service, and/or company.

- Boost **play rate** with a call to action that tells users they can play the video to learn more.

- Create multiple video ads with different opening image sizes to increase the number of places where your ad is eligible to appear (since different websites accept different ad sizes).

- Keep the video engaging and no longer than necessary (play rates drop off significantly after 45 seconds).

- Be clear about business offers.

- Deliver key messages early in the video, because users may not watch the whole thing.

- Provide clear next steps for users to take after finishing the video, such as making a purchase or visiting the website or store.

- Remember to use negative keywords and the site exclusion tool to block ads from showing alongside content that doesn't fit the advertiser's marketing objectives.

Integrating Different Ad Formats into an Ad Campaign

Image and video ads may look different than text ads, but they still must adhere to the same quality and cost principles discussed in earlier lessons. That is, Google ranks image and video ads based on Quality Score and maximum bid.

Image and text ads can be used for both keyword- and site-targeted campaigns. In fact, one ad group can contain any combination of text, image, or video ads. The AdWords system determines whether to show the text ad, image ad, or video ad. If the image ad is more relevant, it will appear. If not, the text ad or video ad may appear in its place. The system is designed so the customer is connected with the most effective ad. This means that the advertiser must monitor ad performance to determine which ads to keep and which ads to improve upon.

Different ad formats require different editorial guidelines. For example, image ads must be family-safe and conform to certain size requirements. Advertisers should check editorial guidelines before submitting an ad.

Activity 4-3
Create a video ad of your own.

1. Start by selecting a small business or any product you wish to advertise. Clear your selection with your instructor.

2. Prepare a 30- to 45-second script for your video ad.

3. Prepare a storyboard, on paper if you wish, detailing the visuals you wish to use to match your video's script.

4. If you have the proper equipment and skills, create your video ad as planned above (optional).

Activity 4-4
1. Write down your responses to the following:

• Explain how image and video ads differ from text ads.

• Describe three different formats for image ads and video ads.

• Explain the advantages of using video and image ads.

• Discuss the principles of creating successful image and video advertising ads.

Key Takeaways

- Google uses similar quality and cost standards in determining whether to show a text ad, image ad, or video ad.

- All ads must conform to certain editorial guidelines.

- It's important for advertisers to monitor performance metrics often.

- Image ads can include both still and animated graphics. They only appear on content sites that have opted into Google's image ad program.

- Video ads are click-to-play ads that appear on sites in the Google Network.

- The key to successful image and video ads is to engage users with images while adhering to the keys to success for text ads (calls to action, accurate description of products and services, focused targeting, etc.).

Vocabulary

- Image ads
- Animated ads
- Pixels
- Video ads
- Click-to-play
- Opening image
- Host
- Stream
- Video feed
- Flash
- Play rate

Google Advertising Professional Exam Preparation

To prepare for the Google Advertising Professional exam, study the following lessons at the AdWords Learning Center (**www.google.com/adwords/learningcenter**):

• Using Different Ad Formats

Helpful Links

Google AdWords Editorial Guidelines:
https://adwords.google.com/support/bin/answer.py?answer=6129

Live Video Ad Demo Page:
http://www.google.com/adwords/videoadsdemo.html

Quiz 4

1. Image ads can be created in _____.

a. Keyword-targeted campaign only
b. Site-targeted campaigns only
c. Keyword and site-targeted campaigns

2. Image and video ads are subject to the same quality scoring maximum bid principles that apply to other ads.

a. True
b. False

3. Video ads are 'click-to-play.' The first thing users see when clicking an ad is:

a. A looping video
b. A box with a large 'play' button
c. A text ad
d. A static image

4. Which of the following formats is unacceptable for an image ad online?

a. .tif
b. .gif
c. .png
d. .jpg

5. Image ads must be family-safe.

a. True
b. False

6. With video ads, an advertiser pays based on which pricing model?

a. Cost-per-click
b. Cost-per-impression
c. Either a or b

7. Google hosts and streams video feeds.

a. True
b. False

Local & Mobile Advertising

Objectives

At the end of this lesson, students should be able to:

- Describe local and mobile ad formats

- Explain how local and mobiles ads work

- Discuss the audience for these ads

- List the benefits and disadvantages of these formats

- Describe the targeting options for mobile ads

Going Local: About Local Business Ads

Local business ads are AdWords ads associated with a specific geographical location. They can appear when a user searches for specific businesses or services in the user's geographic area. This option gives advertisers a good way to reach local customers. For example, a user searching for dentists in Palo Alto, California, might type 'dentist Palo Alto, CA' on Google.com. Like Yellow Page listings, Google displays a list of dentists in or near Palo Alto, as shown in Image 5-1.

Image 5-1: Local results for search 'dentist Palo Alto, CA.'

Local business ads are eligible to appear in two places:

- On **Google Maps** (maps.google.com) in the enhanced manner shown in Image 5-2.

- In the regular text-only format on Google.com and other sites in the Google search network.

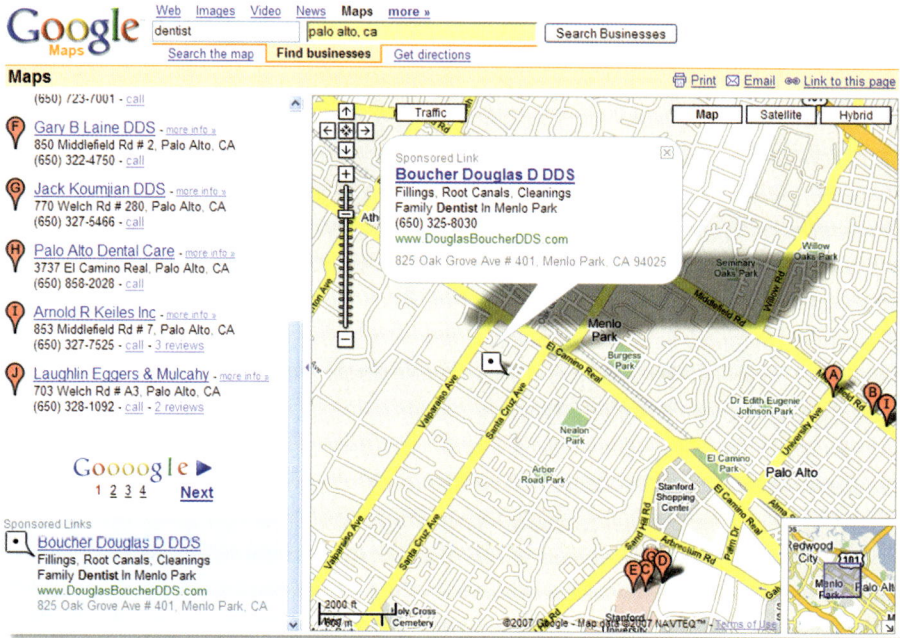

Image 5-2: Local results for search 'dentist Palo Alto, CA.'

Local Business Ads on Google Maps

Google Maps displays an interactive map next to both organic search results and paid AdWords ads. When a user enters a geographic search query, organic search results appear on the left-hand side of the map. Each of these listings is marked in the search results and on the map by a red balloon.

Local business ads appear above or below organic search results, are highlighted by a blue background, and are clearly labeled Sponsored Links. Up to four sponsored listings may appear per search. Each of these listings is marked on the map by a small white balloon. When the ad is clicked, the balloon expands into an **information window** over the physical location of the business on the map (Image 5-2). This larger balloon can contain:

- A headline (25-character maximum)

- Two lines of creative text (35-character maximum per line)

- A small, eye-catching image (125 x 125 pixels)

- A display URL

- The business name and address

Users who click the URL in the ad or in the information window are taken to the advertiser's website.

Local Business Ads on Google.com and the Google Search Network

A text-only version of each local business ad is eligible to run on Google.com and other search sites in the Google search network. The way an ad looks varies by search partner. Typically, ads are labeled as Sponsored Links and include two to four lines of text.

In most cases, text versions of local business ads include the same ad text and display URL as the enhanced ads running on Google Maps. An additional fifth line of text also appears that includes the city and state of the business (if applicable).

Activity 5-1

1. Visit maps.google.com and search on the term 'restaurants' plus your zip code.

2. View the results. Can you differentiate between the ads and organic results? Click an ad. Do you think the copy is effective? Why or why not?

3. Play around with the mapping technology. Zoom in and out, drag the map around, and try different views by clicking on the following tabs:

- map

- satellite

- hybrid

4. Critique your experience.

Getting on the Map: Creating Local Business Ads

Almost anyone in the United States can create a local business listing for free through the **Google Local Business Center** (google.com/local/add); there is no charge to the business to appear on Google Maps. There are two steps AdWords advertisers must take to enable local business ads to run on Google, Google Maps, and search sites in the Google Network:

1. Create a business listing in Google Maps

2. Create AdWords local business ads

Step 1: Create a Local Business Center Listing

Advertisers first need to add their business listing to Google's Local Business Center. Since Google verifies that the business address is correct, it can take several days before a local business ad starts to run. After Google initially verifies the address, advertisers can edit listings as often as they like. Changes are reflected in search results within six weeks.

Step 2: Create Local Business Ads within an AdWords account

From the ad group view of the 'Campaign Summary' page, click 'Create New Local Business Ad' and follow the instructions. Each ad group may contain several local business ads for different locations. There may be multiple local business ads for one business location.

When creating local business ads, follow the guidelines for good text ads. Each local business ad must be associated to a business location within the campaign's targeted region. For example, if an advertiser's campaign targets California, he won't be able to create local business ads for businesses in London. Finally, the headline of the local business ad should accurately reflect the business name as it appears in Google Maps.

Activity 5-2

Create a local business ad for a business you frequent. Include a screen shot.

Mobile Ads: Advertising on the Go

Searchers can see AdWords ads just about anywhere—not just in front of their computer screens. Google shows AdWords ads for searches made on mobile devices, like web-enabled cell phones, smart phones, or personal digital assistants (PDAs). These ads are called **mobile ads**.

Mobile ads are short, text-based AdWords ads that contain two lines of text, with a limit of 12 or 18 characters per line (depending on the language the ad is written in). Users have two options when viewing a mobile ad:

• Click through to the advertiser's mobile webpage (the advertiser's display URL appears in the ad's third line)

Call the business phone listed. A **'Call' link** will appear next to the display URL. The user clicks the link, enters his number, and Google connects the user to the business for free.

Image: 5-3: A mobile ad.

More: A mobile web page is a version of the advertiser's website that is formatted to display on mobile phones. A mobile web page is written in a mobile markup language, such as XHTML, WML, or CHTML.

Mobile ads are available in keyword-targeted campaigns only. Advertisers either pay per click (when users click through to the website) or pay per call (when users click the call link). Mobile ads can only be targeted to a country (not a city or state). Therefore, advertisers should choose geographically targeted keywords (like 'san francisco pizza') when creating mobile ads. Mobile ads are similar to local ads in that advertisers can experiment and create multiple mobile ads per ad group.

More: In 2006, 80 percent of the world's 6 billion people had access to mobile phone service. By 2010, the percentage is expected to increase to 90 percent. (Research commissioned by the Global System for Mobile Association. Reported in the Taipei Times, Wednesday, October 18, 2006.)

Activity 5-3
List three local businesses that might benefit from mobile advertising. Explain why you believe each business can benefit from a mobile advertising campaign.

Activity 5-4
Find a mobile ad using a cell phone or other mobile device for a business you typically visit (like a pizza shop). Describe the experience. Critique the ad. Was it relevant to your search? How much do you think the advertiser would be willing to pay for a click or call on this ad? Explain your reasoning.

Integrating Local with Mobile: Google Maps for Mobile

Google sometimes shows local business ads for relevant searches made on mobile devices (www.google.com/gmm), as shown in Image 5-4. Google Maps for mobile is a mapping program for mobile devices. Since ads that appear in mobile search results contain only two lines of text, local business ads may show in a shortened form on mobile searches. (Currently, advertisers aren't charged for impressions or clicks accrued by local business ads in mobile searches.)

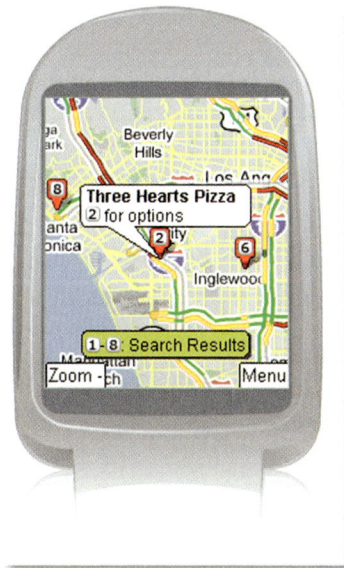

Image 5-4: A local business ad appears on Google Maps for Mobile.

Google Text Messaging

Users can view Google search results using simple messaging service (SMS) text messaging. To use **Google SMS**, users send a text message of a search query to 466453 ('GOOGLE' on most devices). Google runs a search and texts back the results. Some examples of Google SMS queries appear in the table below.

Search Features	Example query
Local Listings	pizza 94040
Movies	Casablanca 94110
Prices	price ipod player 40gb

Text versions of local business ads can also appear in Google SMS query results. Due to the limited amount of space in the SMS format, ad text may not be included in its entirety. However, the advertiser's business name and contact information is included (Image 5-5.)

Image 5-5: An ad shown on Google SMS.

Activity 5-5

Pick three local area businesses and write three separate mobile ads to fit their needs and business models.

Activity 5-6

Review your reading and respond to the following questions and statements:

- Describe the various local and mobile ad formats and discuss the various advantages or disadvantages of these formats.

- Explain how local and mobiles ads work. Discuss how they are helpful to customers (or the audience for mobile ads) as well as helpful to businesses (which place mobile ads).

- How are mobile ads targeted to help specific customers?

Key Takeaways

- Local business ads appear for geographic searches on Google.com and search sites in the Google Network and on Google Maps.

- Local business ads appear under Sponsored Listings above or below organic search results on Google Maps. They're displayed next to a white balloon.

- Local business ads are available for keyword-targeted campaigns only. To post a local business ad, an advertiser must create a business listing using the Google Maps Local Business Center, and then create local business ads.

- Mobile ads are short, text-based AdWords ads that appear when users search Google from a mobile device.

- Users who click a mobile ad either click through to the advertiser's mobile website or click-to-call the business number listed.

- Text versions of local business ads may also appear on mobile devices.

Vocabulary

- Google Maps
- Information window
- Google Local Business Center
- Mobile ads
- Google Maps for Mobile
- Google SMS
- 'Call' link
- Mobile markup language

Google Advertising Professional Exam Preparation

To prepare for the GAP qualification exam, study the following information at the AdWords Learning Center (**www.google.com/adwords/learningcenter**):

- "Local Business Ads"
- "Mobile Ads"

Quiz

1. AdWords Local Business Ads can appear:

a) On Google Maps
b) On Google SMS query results
c) On Google Maps for Mobile
d) On the Google Local Business Center
e) All of the above
f) a, b & c

2. Local Business Ads can contain an image.

a) True
b) False

With mobile ads, you have the choice to:

a) Connect users to your mobile website
b) Connect users to your business phone
c) Use cost-per-click or cost-per-call pricing
d) All of the above

2. Mobile ads contain _____ lines of ad text with a maximum of _____ characters on each line

a) 3, 25 to 35
b) 2, 18 to 25
c) 2, 12 to 25
d) 2, 12 to 18

Tracking Performance

Objectives

At the end of this lesson, students should be able to:

- Gather data to determine if a website and ads are a good investment
- Read AdWords reports
- Evaluate ROI for an advertising program
- Use and interpret AdWords conversion tracking tools
- Use and interpret Google Analytics

Performance Basics: Conversions and ROI Defined

There's an old marketing joke that goes, "I know half my advertising works, I just don't know which half." Advertising is only effective if it generates measurable results for a business. In the past, determining whether an ad was a good investment required a lot of guesswork. Advanced technology now makes it possible to determine when an ad leads to a **conversion**.

Conversions

The term 'conversion' usually refers to turning a non-customer into a customer. If, for example, someone clicks on an AdWords ad and buys something on the associated site, the click counts as a conversion from a site visit to a site sale (the visitor is converted to a customer).

Since different businesses can have different advertising goals, 'conversion' can actually have a variety of meanings. For example, a conversion can refer to any of the following:

- **A purchase**. For example, a visitor purchases a digital camera.

- **A sales lead**. For example, a visitor submits his contact information to get an insurance quote.

- **A download**. For example, a prospective buyer downloads a research paper about a company's software capabilities.

- **A subscription**. For example, a new subscriber completes the sign-up process for a newsletter.

- **A page view**. For example, a visitor looks at an important webpage on a website.

Return on Investment

Return on Investment (ROI) helps an advertiser determine the best way to spend advertising dollars. ROI generally refers to the profit or revenue generated from a specific activity, as a percentage of the money spent on the activity. For example, if an investor buys a stock for $100, and sells it for $110, she's achieved a 10% return on her investment.

In advertising, ROI can also be called **return on ad spend** (ROAS). Advertising ROI is calculated as revenue from sales minus advertising costs, divided by the cost of advertising:

ROI = (Sales Revenue - Advertising Cost) / Advertising Cost

For example, if Pam's advertising costs for the past week were $500 and she's sold $1,000 worth of goods as a result, she has a 100% ROI for the week (to express ROI as a percentage, multiply the result of this formula by 100):

(($1000 – $500) / $500) x 100 = 100%

AdWords and ROI

ROI can be determined for an AdWords ad campaign or for individual keywords in the ad campaign.

AdWords posts advertising costs for a specific time period in the account Campaign Summary statistics. Sales revenue is simply the total value of sales for the same time period. The ROI can then be calculated:

((Sales Revenue – Advertising Cost) / Advertising Cost) x 100.

To determine ROI for individual keywords, consider the following example. Arthur owns a camera shop that sells photography equipment and photography classes. He chooses to advertise using the keywords 'photo equipment' and 'photography classes,' as shown in Table 6-1.

Arthur's daily budget is $100. On average, the keyword 'photo equipment' generates 110 clicks, resulting in $120 in sales, and costs Arthur $75 a day. This results in a 60% ROI for the keyword 'photo equipment': (($120 – $75) / $75) x 100.

The keyword 'photography classes' uses only $25 of his total $100 daily advertising budget. However, it generates 40 clicks. These clicks result in $90 in sales, generating an ROI of 260%: (($90 – $25) / $25) x 100.

Even though 'photography classes' results in fewer clicks than 'photo equipment,' Arthur should allocate more of his budget to 'photography classes.' He can do this by increasing the maximum CPC bid for 'photography classes' while decreasing his maximum CPC bid for 'photo equipment.'

Keyword	Clicks	Cost	Sales	Revenue Minus Cost	ROI
Photo equipment	110	$75/day	$120/day	$60	100%
Photography classes	40	$25/day	$90/day	$65	260%

Table 6-1: In this example, the keyword 'photography classes' earns a greater ROI than the keyword 'photo equipment.' This advertiser should allocate a greater amount of his advertising budget to 'photography classes.'

Activity 6-1

You own an online photography store and also offer web-based photography classes. Your budget is $150/day. You know the following data:

Keyword	Max CPC	Clicks	Cost	Sales	CPC	Revenue Minus Cost	ROI
Photography equipment	$0.75	145	$70/day	$120/day			
Photography classes	$0.75	50	$35/day	$100/day			

1. Complete the table above.

2. How would you change your maximum CPC bid to increase your profit? Justify your answer.

3. You suspect that people who take your classes also buy photography equipment from you. How would this affect your answer to question 2? How might you track this? How would you adjust your ROI calculation?

More: What if the cost of acquiring a customer is more than the revenue the customer generates? Spending too much on advertising can be a good way to go out of business. However, in some cases, **lifetime customer-value** may be greater than the cost of the acquisition. That is, because of repeat business, a customer may become profitable on the second or third visit.

Quick Performance Tracking: Campaign Summary Metrics and the Report Center

There are two ways to quickly glean AdWords performance data: through metrics on the Campaign Summary page and through the Report Center.

Campaign Summary Metrics

AdWords provides the following information on the Campaign Summary page:

Clicks

Clicks are the basic measure of success of an AdWords ad. Successful keywords are relevant and generate a lot of clicks at a low CPC. However, clicks can be deceiving. Clicks may just be a sign that people are curious about an ad; people may click on an ad frequently, but rarely turn into customers.

Click-through Rate (CTR)

Keywords with high CTRs may indicate that a keyword and ad are giving people what they want – and leading to conversions. But again, a high CTR is no guarantee of conversions or ROI.

Impressions

If generating awareness for a brand is important, the number of impressions can be a sign of success.

AdWords Reports

AdWords reports (located in an advertiser's 'Reports' tab) generate customized performance data for multiple facets of an AdWords account. Key features include:

- Performance stats for site/keyword campaigns, URLs, ad groups, and the account

- Customizable report columns to focus a report on only relevant data

- Performance filters to screen for the most relevant information in categories such as cost, impressions, clicks, and CTR

- Simple scheduling to automatically generate reports and deliver them to multiple recipients

- The ability to create report templates for reuse

Level of Detail : These columns reflect this report's coverage and level of detail

| ☑ Campaign | ☑ Ad Group | ☑ Site / Keyword |

Attributes : These columns report on your current ad settings and status

☐ Ad Distribution	☐ Campaign Status	☐ Daily Budget
☐ Ad Group Status	☑ Keyword Status	☑ Match Type
☑ Keyword Destination URL	☐ Content Bid	☑ Keyword Min CPC
☑ Current Maximum CPC	☑ Current Maximum CPM	☐ Highest Position Preference
☐ Lowest Position Preference		

Performance Statistics : These columns feature data about how your ads are performing

☑ Clicks	☑ Impressions	☑ CTR
☑ Avg CPC	☑ Avg CPM	☑ Cost
☑ Avg Position		

Conversion Columns : These columns provide statistics on ad conversions and conversion rates

☐ Conversions	☐ Transactions	☐ Conversion Rate
☐ Cost/conversion	☐ Cost/transaction	☐ Total Value
☐ Avg Value	☐ Value/cost	☐ Value/click
☐ Sales Count	☐ Leads Count	☐ Sign-up Count
☐ Sales Value	☐ Leads Value	☐ Sign-up Value
☐ Page View Count	☐ Page View Value	☐ Other Count
☐ Other Value		

Image 6-1: Some of the data you can include in custom reports.

Topic 3

AdWords Conversion Tracking

AdWords' conversion tracking tool shows how many conversions result from an advertiser's AdWords ads. To start conversion tracking, AdWords provides a code snippet that the advertiser includes in the HTML of the conversion page. Conversion tracking automatically places a cookie on a user's computer when the user clicks on an ad. If the user reaches a specified conversion page (by making a purchase, signing up for a newsletter, etc.), then:

1) The user's browser sends the cookie to a Google server

2) Google records a successful conversion

3) A small conversion tracking image is displayed on the advertiser's site

4) The conversion data is presented within the Campaign Summary section of the advertiser's account

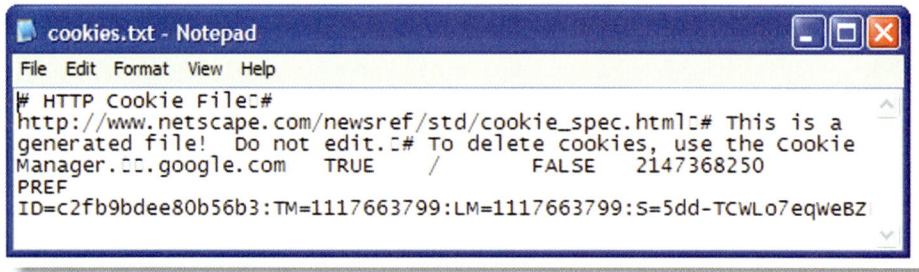

```
cookies.txt - Notepad
File  Edit  Format  View  Help
# HTTP Cookie File:#
http://www.netscape.com/newsref/std/cookie_spec.html:# This is a
generated file!  Do not edit.:# To delete cookies, use the Cookie
Manager.::.google.com    TRUE    /        FALSE    2147368250
PREF
ID=c2fb9bdee80b56b3:TM=1117663799:LM=1117663799:S=5dd-TCWLo7eqweBZ
```

Image 6-2: An example of a cookie shown in Notepad. A cookie is a small text file containing data such as user ID, user preferences, shopping cart information, or other information.

More: Does Google know what I buy on the Internet? No. Google uses different computers for conversion tracking and search results. The cookie Google adds to a user's computer when he clicks on an ad disappears in 30 days.

Conversion Statistics

The following conversion tracking statistics are available in AdWords accounts. They can also be used to generate reports in the Report Center:

of conversions

A conversion is counted when an ad click leads to a user taking a specified action on a site. Multiple conversions from a single ad click are counted as only one conversion. Conversions are only counted from ads on Google and some of Google's network partners. The conversion rate is adjusted to reflect only the ad clicks for which Google can track conversions.

Average value

The total value of all conversions divided by the total number of conversions.

Conversion types

The type of conversion recorded (purchase/sale, signup, page view, lead, or self-defined/customized). The advertiser specifies which type of conversion has occurred.

Conversion rate

The number of conversions divided by the number of eligible ad clicks.

Cost/conversion

The total cost of ad clicks divided by the total number of conversions. This statistic gives the amount spent per conversion.

Transaction

A single occurrence of a conversion event. Multiple transactions can occur after a user clicks on an ad. For example, a user clicks on Arthur's ad and makes two separate purchases on his site, one worth $11 and one worth $12. AdWords informs Arthur that one conversion has resulted from the ad, as well as two purchase transactions, for a total value of $23. A lead generation can also be considered a transaction, e.g. if a visitor fills out a form and provides particular information that the advertiser deems valuable.

Cost/transaction

The total cost of ad clicks divided by the total number of transactions. This statistic gives the average amount spent on advertising per transaction. Transactions are counted only for conversions from Google and some of Google's network sites. The cost per transaction is adjusted to reflect only the cost of ad clicks on which Google can track conversions.

Monitoring Conversions

Conversion rate and cost-per-conversion are important statistics to monitor; however, each individual conversion can lead to multiple transactions as users shop for various products on a site or return later to make additional purchases. Transaction and cost-per-transaction statistics show how advertisers can acquire regular customers (who are usually more valuable than any single conversion). Transaction statistics can provide valuable insight into the effectiveness of advertising, the site, and the product offerings.

More: How accurate is conversion tracking? Google conversion tracking has a few limitations. Because the tracking code is a JavaScript function associated with a cookie, Internet users who have disabled cookies or JavaScript in their browsers won't be tracked. For this reason, multiplying the number of clicks received by conversion rate may not be an accurate way to calculate the number of conversions. In reports, clicks that can't be tracked aren't included in conversion data.

Activity 6-1

Review the following ad group data:

Ad Group Name	Status	Default Bid Max CPC	Clicks	Impr.	CTR	Avg. CPC	Cost	Avg. Pos	Conv. Rate	Cost/Conv. ▼
Brand	Active	$1.00	29,708	600,656	4.94%	$0.28	$8,375.14	1.7	0.14%	$203.65

What is the minimum sales amount necessary to have a positive ROI for this ad group?

Activity 6-2

1. In your own words, define ROI.

2. In your own words, define a conversion.

3. Explain the difference between a transaction and a conversion.

4. What is Cost/conversion in an AdWords account?

5. In your own words, define a cookie.

Cross-Channel Conversion Tracking

Google's **cross-channel conversion tracking** gives conversion data for all online **advertising channels** – not just Google AdWords. These other channels might include other pay-per-click ads, email campaigns, or banner ads. The process for recording a cross-channel conversion is similar to that for recording an AdWords conversion. Cross-channel tracking statistics appear in an AdWords account on a separate 'Cross-Channel' tab on the Campaign Summary page.

The following are important cross-channel tracking terms.

Channel

A network or service which advertisers use to create online ads to be displayed on web pages or elsewhere. Google AdWords is a channel, as are banners, other CPC ads, and email campaigns. The channel types are PPC (pay-per-click) and non-PPC.

Channel ad

A non-AdWords ad an advertiser wants to track using Google's cross-channel tracking tool.

Channel account

An advertising account with another non-AdWords online advertising channel, such as Yahoo! Search Marketing, Lycos, or LookSmart.

Channel campaign

A shell, or mock, campaign created specifically in an AdWords account to track the ROI and other advertising information for ads running on a non-AdWords channel. Channel campaigns usually include one destination URL and one or more keywords.

Tracking URLs

A tracking URL tells you exactly where clicks come from. These are URLs that have identifying information tacked on the end that provide information about the source of the click, the search query used, and other advertising metrics. Tracking URLs help advertisers determine the effectiveness of their ads and/or keywords on non-AdWords channels.

Google tracking URLs

The URLs Google generates for advertisers in the cross-channel setup wizard, which provide information about advertising effectiveness.

How Cross-Channel Tracking Works

In order to use cross-channel tracking, an AdWords advertiser should have access to the website's code. Before setup, the advertiser must have an active ad campaign through another (non-AdWords) online advertising channel.

Google provides a tracking URL (or URLs) for each channel campaign that is set up, which the advertiser uses as the destination URL (or URLs) for the other channels' ad (or ads). When someone clicks on an ad in a non-AdWords channel, Google places a cookie on the user's computer. This cookie sends information to the advertiser's account about how the person found his ad, as well as other details such as the specific keyword-query entered.

Google provides detailed ROI and conversion information for all campaigns. This information gives advertisers the ability to make more informed decisions about where to invest ad dollars.

Google Analytics: Advanced Tracking

Google Analytics is a tool that advertisers use for gathering all kinds of data about their website and their ads. Web analytics software shows advertisers how users found their site and what they do while they're there. By skillfully analyzing reports, an advertiser can:

- Increase conversions
- Improve ROI
- Potentially enhance the visitor's experience
- Improve e-commerce revenue

The 'Analytics' tab (shown in Image 6-3) in an AdWords account provides over 80 reports for different people involved in running a website, such as marketers, web developers, and management.

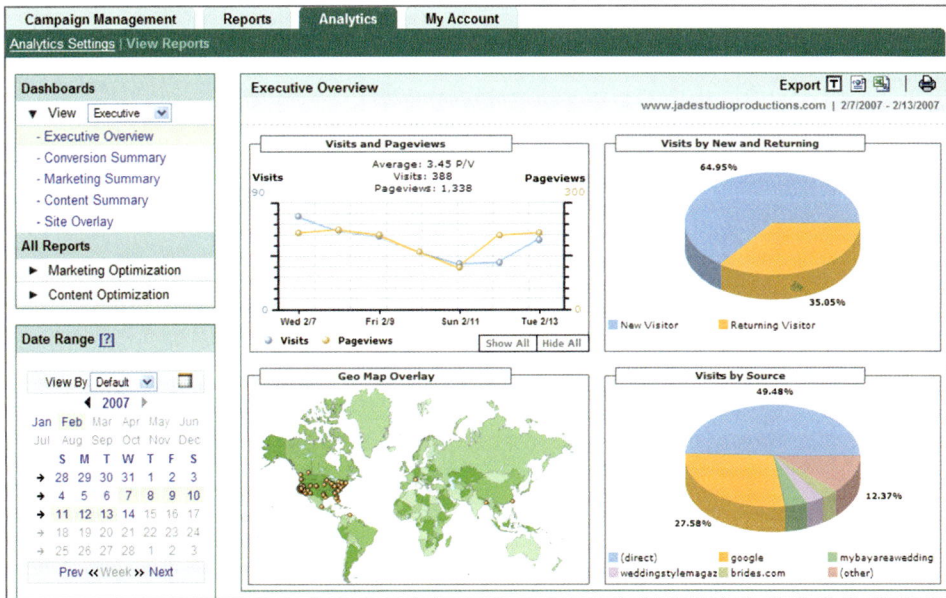

Image 6-3: The Executive Overview, shown here, is one of more than 80 reports found under the 'Analytics' tab of an AdWords account.

Google Analytics provides reports on:

- How many new and returning visitors come to a website
- Where visitors live in the world
- How users find a website (called referring sources)
- How visitors navigate and use a website
- Sales trends
- How sales relate to ads
- E-commerce metrics such as revenue and conversion rates

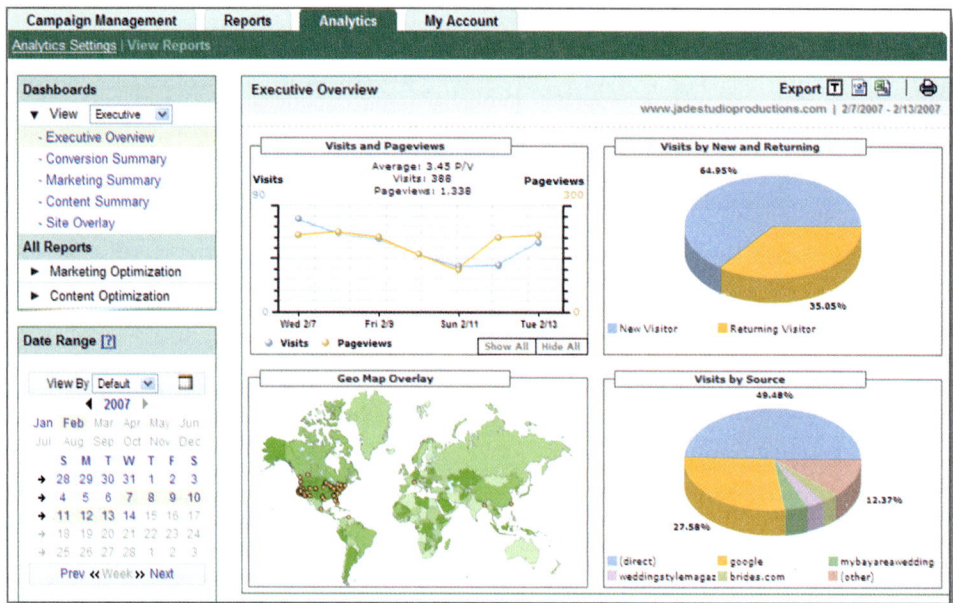

Image 6-4: Google Analytics can help marketers answer their most difficult questions through reports that address the topics above

Activity 6-3
Write a paragraph, in your own words, describing the information provided in the Executive Overview report in Image 6-4.

Deeper Analysis

Some Analytics reports provide the option to analyze individual lines of data. The Analysis Options icon ⬢ gives the advertiser the option to look at:

- **Data Over Time:** includes the values for the selected report over a selected date range

- **Overlay Page:** loads the Site Overlay report for the selected page

- **To-date Lifetime Value:** calculates that page's values from when Analytics tracking began

- **Cross Segment Performance:** looks at a report's data in detail by a specified variable (segment)

For example, the **Source ROI** report (Image 6-5) shows that **google[organic]** (that is, Google search results) is the second highest **source** of visits to this website.

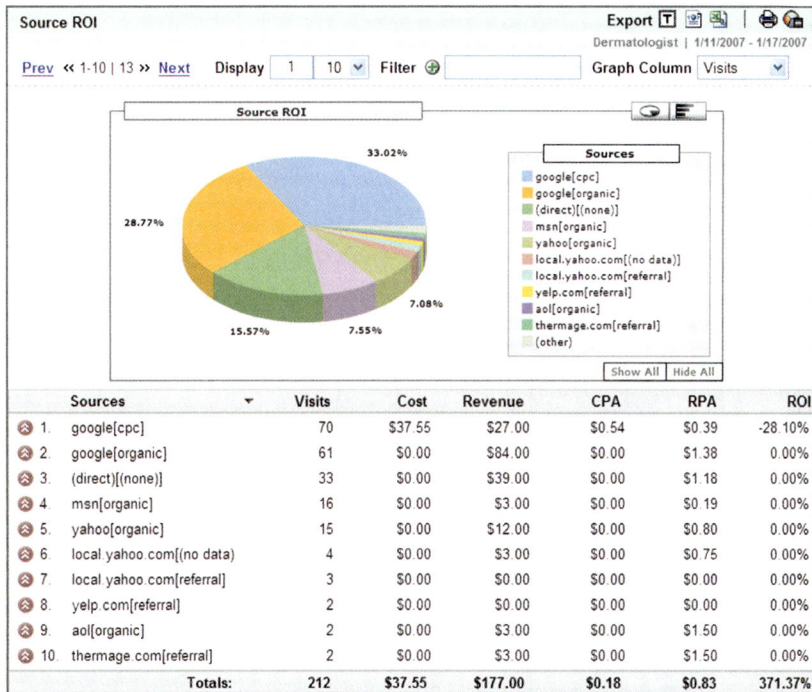

Image 6-5: The Google Analytics Source ROI report.

The following choices appear when the Analysis Options icon ⊗ licked.

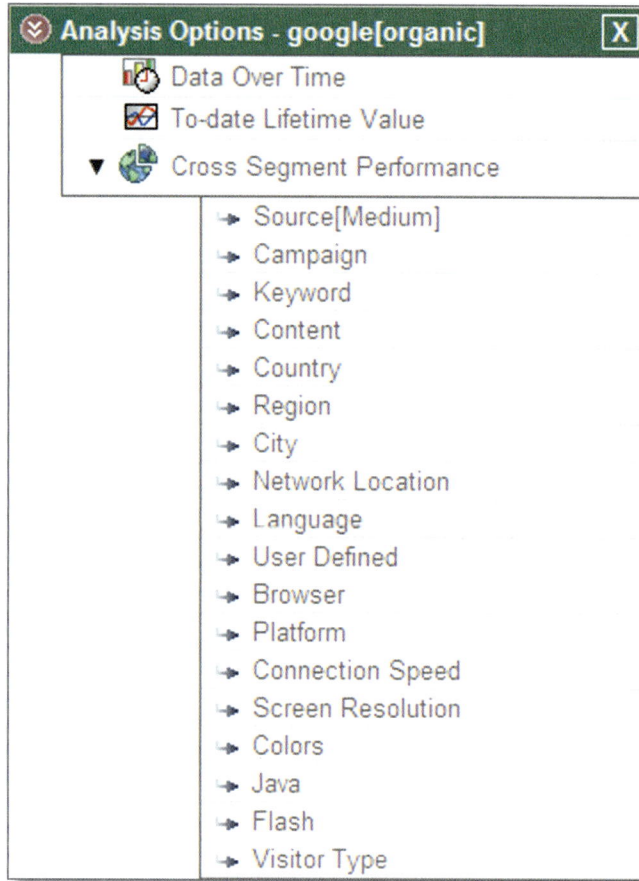

Image 6-6: The Google Analytics analysis options.

When 'Cross Segment Performance > Keyword' is clicked (Image 6-7), the report changes to show the keywords that brought the most users to the website.

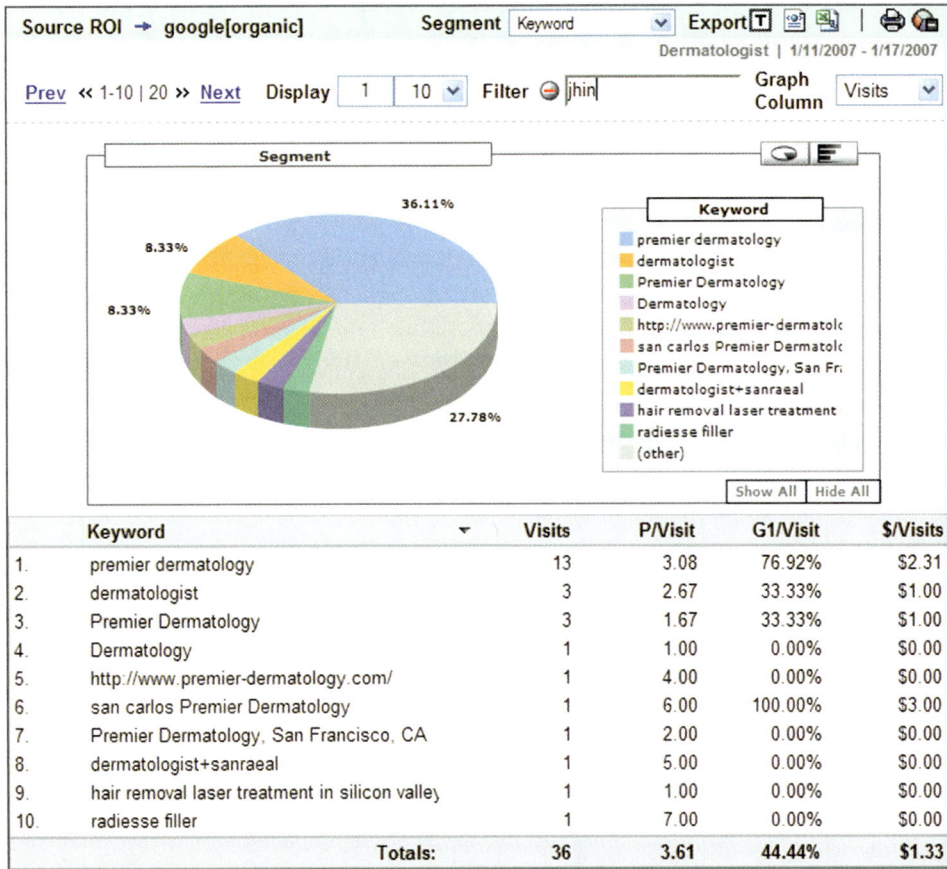

	Keyword	Visits	P/Visit	G1/Visit	$/Visits
1.	premier dermatology	13	3.08	76.92%	$2.31
2.	dermatologist	3	2.67	33.33%	$1.00
3.	Premier Dermatology	3	1.67	33.33%	$1.00
4.	Dermatology	1	1.00	0.00%	$0.00
5.	http://www.premier-dermatology.com/	1	4.00	0.00%	$0.00
6.	san carlos Premier Dermatology	1	6.00	100.00%	$3.00
7.	Premier Dermatology, San Francisco, CA	1	2.00	0.00%	$0.00
8.	dermatologist+sanraeal	1	5.00	0.00%	$0.00
9.	hair removal laser treatment in silicon valley	1	1.00	0.00%	$0.00
10.	radiesse filler	1	7.00	0.00%	$0.00
	Totals:	36	3.61	44.44%	$1.33

Image 6-7: The Google Analytics Source ROI report, cross-segmented by keyword.

Activity 6-4
List the ways you can cross segment a report.

Tracking ROI Across Multiple Ad Campaigns – Online and Offline

AdWords provides multiple tools for tracking online ad campaigns. But what if an advertiser also advertises offline (such as in newspapers or flyers)? Here are some alternative ways to gather useful performance data across different campaigns:

Promotional Code

A promotional code can be useful to pinpoint exactly from where a sale comes. For example, a newspaper ad might say, "Mention promotional code 'Valentine' when you make your appointment and get 10% off." Or an AdWords ad might say, "Use code web1 for 10% off." In this way, an advertiser can track which ads generate the most business.

Multiple Phone Lines

An advertiser with multiple phone lines can place different phone numbers in different ads. For example, he may put:

• Phone Line 1 in his business listing in the phone book for regular business calls

• Phone Line 2 in a newspaper ad

• Phone Line 3 on the website

In this way, the advertiser knows which source is generating calls.

Tracking URLs

You can place a tracking URL anywhere. For example, in a newspaper ad, you can promote a unique web page URL that is not advertised anywhere else. In this way, you know that all the traffic to that web page originated from that newspaper ad.

Activity 6-5

An eye doctor spends $5,000 in one year to bring 10,000 visitors to her website. In the same year, the doctor spends $5,000 on an ad in a local weekly newspaper. Discuss the limitations and advantages of each type of advertising. Describe how you might track each type of advertising.

Activity 6-6

Find a local newspaper ad with a promotional code. Critique it. Include the ad with your write-up. Does the ad include a reference to a website? If so, is the reference effective? If not, how might it be changed to be more effective?

Activity 6-7

In your own words:

1. Explain what conversion tracking does.

2. Explain what web analytics software does.

3. Describe how you might track offline ads.

Google Checkout – Don't Lose Your Customers at the Last Step of the Sale

Often, when using analytics software, advertisers learn that a lot of potential customers put items in their shopping cart, but leave before completing the sale (called shopping cart abandonment). Lengthy checkout processes frustrate online shoppers. Google Checkout enables customers to complete a purchase quickly, sometimes with a single click. This feature can greatly increase your conversion rate.

More: Google Checkout is kind of like having a free cash-register for your online store.

Merchants can use Checkout to charge customers' credit cards, process their orders, and receive payments in their bank account. Google Checkout also offers **fraud protection** to the buyer and merchant. If you're a small merchant, you can use Checkout to create a 'Buy Now' button that you can place on any product website. If you're a large merchant, you can integrate your current website, shopping cart, and order processing system with Google Checkout.

Key Takeaways

- ROI and conversions are two ways to determine an ad's performance.

- A 'conversion' can refer to a sale, a lead, a page view, a signup, and more.

- ROI calculation is ((Sales Revenue – Advertising Cost) / Advertising Cost) x 100.

- Advertisers can view performance stats quickly via their Campaign Summary page or by running a report.

- AdWords conversion tracking gives conversion stats for AdWords campaigns. It requires special setup.

- Cross-channel tracking compares data across multiple online campaigns, not just for AdWords accounts.

- Web analytics software provides advanced performance metrics for analyzing an ad campaign.

Vocabulary

- Conversion
- Return on investment
- Return on ad spend (ROAS)
- Lifetime customer-value
- Conversion tracking
- Code snippet
- Cookie
- Conversion page
- Transaction
- Total value
- Cross-channel conversion tracking
- Advertising channel
- Channel type
- Code snippet
- Advertising channels
- Google Analytics
- Web analytics software
- Tracking URL
- Tracking URL parameters
- Cross segment
- Source
- Referring source
- Google Checkout
- Shopping cart abandonment
- Fraud protection

Google Advertising Professional Exam Preparation

To prepare for the Google Advertising Professional exam, study the following information at the AdWords Learning Center (**www.google.com/adwords/learningcenter**):

• Google Analytics

• Tracking Ad Performance

• Account Performance Tools

• Analtyics Tools

Helpful Links

Google Cross Channel Conversion Tracking Guide:
https://adwords.google.com/select/crosschannel.html

Google Analytics Conversion University:
http://www.google.com/analytics/conversionuniversity.html

Google Checkout Demonstration:
http://checkout.google.com/seller/demo.html

Google Checkout Badge Demonstration:
http://checkout.google.com/seller/demo_badge.html

Quiz 6

1. An advertiser spends $20 for clicks on a keyword, resulting in $100 in sales. What is the ROI for this keyword?

a. 500%
b. 400%
c. 40%
d. 125%

2. ROAS is an acronym for _____.

a. revenue of ad spend
b. return on ad space
c. return on ad spend
d. return on ad stock

3. An advertiser sells chocolates with Google AdWords. Given the conversion data below, what is the minimum amount that she must charge per sale to earn a profit?

Keyword	Clicks	Impr.	CTR	Avg. CPC	Cost	Conv. Rate	Cost/Conv.
chocolate	222	1,922	11.5%	$1.05	$230.95	6.31%	$16.50

a. $1.06
b. $16.51
c. $16.64
d. $230.96

4. Cost-per-acquisition (CPA) can be a measure of advertising effectiveness.

a. True
b. False

5. To install Google Analytics on your website, the best place to add the snippet of JavaScript is _____.

a. on the conversion, or "thank you," page of your site
b. in the HTML body of each page on your site
c. in the HTML head of each page on your site
d. in the HTML body of your homepage

The Future of AdWords Advertising

Detailed Objectives

At the end of this lesson, students should be able to:

- Discuss potential features for online search marketing

- Explain pricing methods that may be used in the future

- Describe possibilities for incorporating offline media into ad campaigns

The Changing AdWords Landscape

Search advertising is constantly changing, so advertisers should constantly stay abreast of new developments in the industry and in online advertising programs. In 2006, for example, AdWords introduced dozens of new features, including:

- **Position preference:** Lets advertisers pick the position in which their ads show on a given page (top spot, second spot, third spot, etc.).

- **Ad scheduling:** Provides control over the days and times ads are shown.

- **AdWords Editor:** An application for making bulk edits across an AdWords account while offline.

AdWords has many new features in store for the future. Here's a quick glimpse at what the future beholds. (Please note that Google is constantly testing new products. Therefore, ad formats and features discussed in this lesson may not be implemented.)

Different Pricing Models

Some new pricing models that have been discussed include:

- **Pay-per-action:** Advertisers pay only for actions that they've defined, such as the generation of a lead or the completion of a sale.

- **Pay-per-call (or click-to-call):** Advertisers pay for calls that their online ads generate. Currently Google is testing this pricing model (Image 7-1). Click-to-call enables users to make a free call to businesses they find on Google search results.

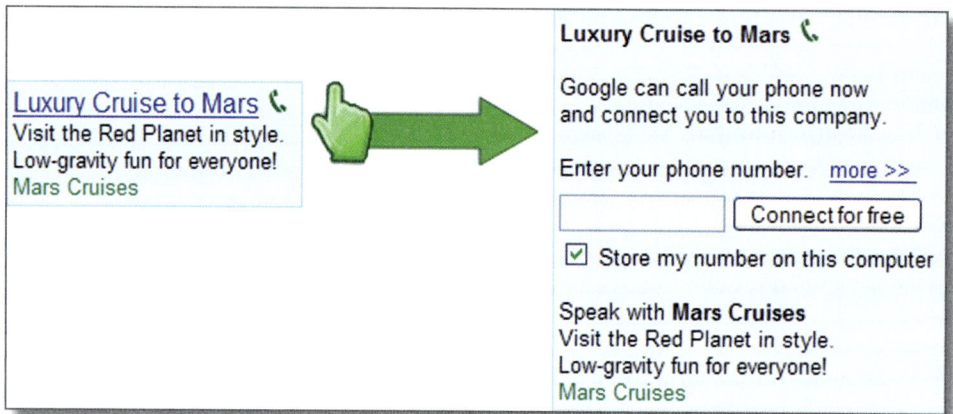

Image 7-1: The experimental AdWords click-to-call format.

New Ad Formats

Much of **ad inventory** goes unsold. For example:

- **Print:** newspapers could print additional ads if there were advertisers who were ready to buy the ad space.

- **Audio:** Many radio stations have time in their schedule for more ads than are sold.

Google hopes to make these offline mediums available to advertisers who previously couldn't afford them, didn't have access to them, or just never considered them.

- Audio ads: Let advertisers target radio listeners by demographic, time of day, or radio station type – for hundreds of radio stations across the U.S. Online reports provide details of when and where ads are played.

- Print ads: Let advertisers select, schedule, deliver, and automatically track their newspaper and magazine ad campaigns. Contextual placement may also be a new twist for print ads.

- Video and in-stream ads: Sites like YouTube.com and Google Video may be the future of TV. Users can upload and watch both amateur and professional videos. Google intends to share advertising proceeds with the publishers of these videos. In-stream ads will be blended into videos seamlessly, just like on TV.

Query: What is a Beta Test? A beta test is when a select audience uses an experimental product to assess the potential success of a product. It is preceded by an alpha test.

Activity 71

Can you dream up a feature? As online marketing evolves, new products and features will be requested and discussed. Open your Internet browser and visit the Inside AdWords blog at http://adwords.blogspot.com/, then answer the following questions:

1. What is the most recent new feature that you can find?

2. What is the benefit of this feature for Google AdWords advertisers?

3. What is the benefit of this feature for Google users?

4. If you were an advertiser, what feature or ad format would you request?

Key Takeaways

- New features are added to Google AdWords and to other search advertising programs regularly. Advertisers and search advertising managers should stay abreast of these developments.

- New pricing models may include pay-per-action or pay-per-call advertising.

- New technology may give advertisers the ability to target offline media, like radio and print advertising.

Vocabulary

- Position preference
- Ad scheduling
- AdWords Editor
- Click-to-Call
- Pay-per-action
- Beta Test
- Audio Ads
- Print Ads
- Google Video
- In-stream video ads

Google Advertising Professional Exam Preparation

To prepare for the Google Advertising Professional exam, study the following lessons at the AdWords Learning Center (**www.google.com/adwords/learningcenter**):

- AdWords Editor
- Cost Control

Helpful Links

The Inside AdWords blog – learn more about AdWords news and product releases: **http://adwords.blogspot.com/**

Search Engine Watch:
searchenginewatch.com

Webmaster World:
www.webmasterworld.com

Quiz 7

1. What is position preference?

a. The option to guarantee a desired position for your ad
b. The option to select a specific partner website for your ad to show on
c. The option to select a desired position from the top of a page for your ad
d. The option to show your ad in the search results

2. Ad scheduling enables advertisers to choose the time during the day they would like their ads to show.

a. True
b. False

3. What is pay-per-action bidding?

a. Advertisers pay only when their ad is clicked on sites in the content network
b. Advertisers pay only for clicks that lead to actions that they've defined, such as a lead generation or a sale
c. Users pay a fee when they purchase an advertiser's product online
d. None of the above

4. Pay-per-call advertising is when a user pays to call an advertiser.

a. True
b. False

AdSense

Detailed Objectives

After completing this lesson, students should be able to:

- Describe AdSense and who can benefit from AdSense advertising
- Describe AdSense for Content
- Describe AdSense for Search
- Explain how AdSense accounts are created
- Explain how AdSense ads are incorporated into a web page

AdSense Overview

Google AdSense is a way for website owners to earn money by displaying relevant, unobtrusive Google ads. The program gives publishers a way to **monetize** (or make money from) and enhance page content. AdSense targets ads to match the content on a publishers' site. AdSense ads can add value to a site by putting interested visitors together with relevant products.

For instance, Apartment Ratings (www.apartmentratings.com) gives apartment seekers information about apartments in specific geographic areas. The Google ads shown in image 8-1 help Apartment Ratings monetize its efforts and support its goal of providing a valuable service to apartment hunters.

Image 8-1: AdWords ads shown on ApartmentRatings.com (outlined in red), an AdSense advertising partner.

The AdSense program offers many benefits to content publishers. First, Google delivers only relevant ads. Second, content providers don't need to negotiate separate advertising arrangements with multiple advertisers – the best ads appear automatically. Third, AdSense gives publishers control over the types of ads that appear. Content publishers can:

- Choose from nearly 2 dozen different formats, sizes, and styles of ads

- Control the color schemes of their ads

- Decide which types of ads they want (or don't want) displayed

- Target ads to a specific geographic area such as California, Norway, or South America

- Choose to display local advertising from area businesses

- Decide which languages are used for ads

AdSense Programs: Content & Search

AdSense for Content

AdSense for Content allows publishers to display ads targeted to a site's specific content (as shown in Image 8-1). Visitors see ads relating to their personal interests. Content providers earn revenue for both CPC and CPM ads. For CPC ads, content publishers are paid when interested users click the ad. For CPM ads, content publishers are paid whenever the ad appears on their page.

AdSense for Search

AdSense for Search allows publishers to place a Google search box on their site (Image 8-2). Visitors can search the Web from the website, or search within the publisher 's web site. The search results appear on the publisher's web pages, as shown in Image 8-3. Publishers earn revenue when a user clicks an ad that appears on the search results page. Publishers don't earn revenue just from the display of an ad, however.

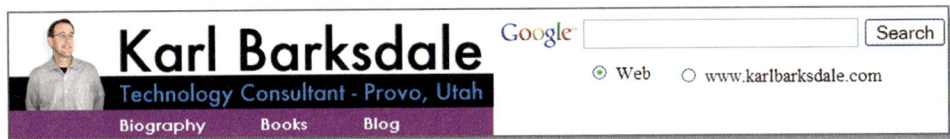

Image 8-2: AdSense gives web publishers a search box they can place on their website.

Image 8-3: AdSense for search gives publishers sponsored ads and organic search results. The ads are shown here outlined in red, and the search results from the publisher's website are outlined in green.

More: SafeSearch is a feature of AdSense for search that blocks explicit adult ads and web pages from appearing on publishers' search results pages.

How AdWords and AdSense Work Together

AdWords advertisers and AdSense publishers have an interdependent relationship. AdWords advertisers provide relevant and valuable ads to AdSense publishers. AdSense publishers provide a highly relevant location for AdWords advertisers to reach targeted and interested customers. When a publisher signs up with AdSense, they become part of Google's content network. The bigger the network gets, the more options AdWords advertisers have on which to show their ads.

Setting Up an AdSense Account

Web publishers can apply to participate in the AdSense program at **www.google.com/adsense**. An ad unit is a portion of a web page dedicated to an advertisement. AdSense publishers can place up to three ad units and one link unit on any page. The size of an ad unit matches the available sizes of image ads (leaderboard, banner, etc.). After a publisher chooses an ad unit, Google provides a code snippet to install in the HTML of the web page where the publisher wants ads to appear. The code enables Google to analyze the site and to match it to relevant ads. Once the new page code is implemented, Google starts displaying ads.

Activity 8-1

1. Visit **www.google.com/adsense**.

2. Choose the Quick Tour link.

3. List three things you learned about AdSense by viewing the Quick Tour.

    1. _____

    2. _____

    3. _____

Tips for Placing AdSense Ads

Generally, ads work best if they're placed above the fold. The phrase "above the fold" comes from the newspaper industry, and refers to papers that are folded in half. On a web page, the term refers to content appearing toward the top left of the web page – so above-the-fold ads are those visitors can see without having to scroll down the page. Some designers choose to emphasize their content more than ads, and so display ads only below the fold.

Here are some other tips to remember about placing ads on a website:

- Try different ad formats to see which ones work best.

- Customize color combinations. Generally, blended sites, where ads' color schemes match (or "blend" with) the design and colors of the website, result in more successful advertising than do sites where ads are in colors that contrast sharply with the site's colors.

- Make sure the Google crawler can index the site. Google needs to analyze each site for keywords to help match them to relevant ads. (Learn more at **www.google.com/webmasters/**)

- Using the AdSense tools, filter out ads that don't add value. For example, a publisher may not want a competitor's ads to appear on its site.

- Provide text-rich pages with interesting content for visitors. A landing page that is "all advertisements all the time" will turn visitors off.

- Keep web pages clean and simple.

Activity 8-2: Designing a Website for AdSense

1. Brainstorm a website that would be of interest to a segment of people. What kind of website or blog would interest a specific, targeted group of individuals? It could be a site dedicated to a sport, an activity, or some academic pursuit. Your site must conform to AdSense policies. AdSense publishers cannot display or promote:

- adult content

- gambling

- prescription or illegal drugs

- tobacco

- firearms

- scams or hoaxes

2. Sketch out a website with the content you brainstormed in step 1. As you design your website, specify the placement of ads in the page design. Explain why you chose the space for each ad unit.

Topic 3

Payment & Reports

AdSense publishers share advertising revenue with Google. New AdSense partners are paid within 30 days after their revenue first reaches $100.

Publishers can view their earnings and other information at any time through their account's Reports tab. Available information includes page and ad unit impressions, ad clicks, click-through rates, and total earnings.

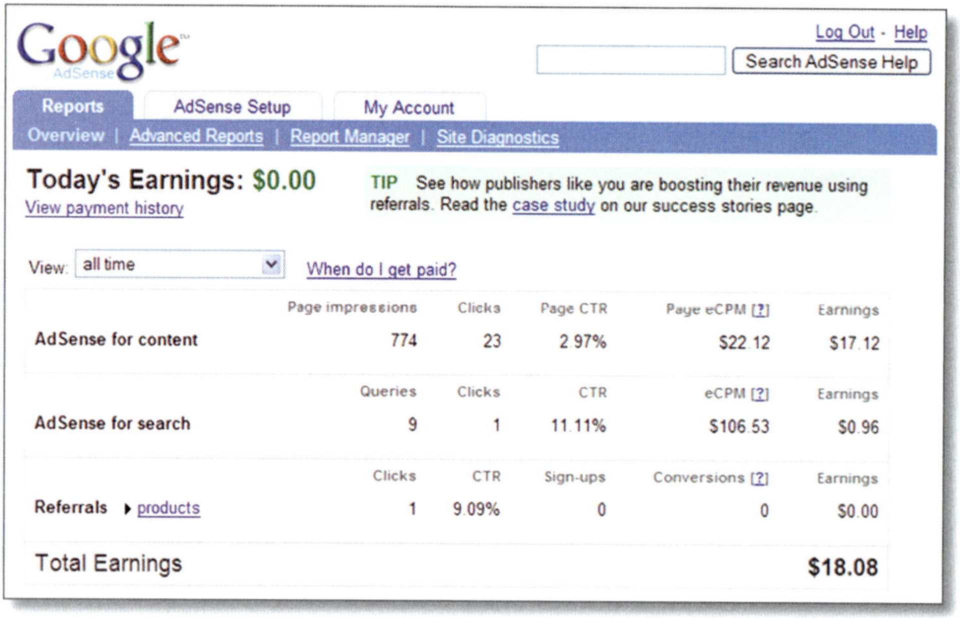

Image 8-4: An AdSense report.

More: AdSense publishers must not click ads that appear on their sites. This maintains a fair environment for advertisers and publishers alike.

Activity 8-3: View a Report and Answer Questions

1. View the report in Image 8-4 and answer the questions below.

a. How much was made from AdSense for Content? AdSense for Search?

b. How many page impressions have appeared on this publisher's site?

c. How many searches have been conducted?

d. Is this AdSense publisher eligible for payment at this moment? Why or why not?

Key Takeaways

- AdSense allows online publishers to make money (monetize their content) by displaying Google Ads.

- AdSense is a mass-market advertising-serving system that generates ad revenue for site publishers.

- SafeSearch filters out inappropriate content from AdSense for Search queries.

- AdWords and AdSense work together to benefit publishers and advertisers.

- AdSense partners can customize ad units by using color schemes, formats, and size to fit the style and content of their websites.

- Publishers are paid after certain earning thresholds have been reached.

Vocabulary

- Monetize
- Above the fold
- Ad Unit
- AdSense for Content
- AdSense for Search
- AdSense referrals
- Electronic funds transfer (EFT)
- Holds
- Publishers
- SafeSearch

Helpful Links

The AdSense Sign-up
www.google.com/adsense/

The AdSense Blog
adsense.blogspot.com/

The AdSense Help Center
www.google.com/adsense/support/

Quiz:

1. To monetize a website means:

a. To have highly targeted advertisements
b. To make money from it
c. To limit the content of a site to a single topic
d. To emphasize one advertisement over all others

2. Which of the following is NOT an accurate statement about AdSense?

a. AdSense tries to put relevant ads on web pages
b. The publisher can control the size and types of ads that appear on its site
c. AdSense ads can target geographical areas
d. AdSense ads are English-only in the United States

3. AdSense does not allow small online publishers.

a. True
b. False

4. AdSense only allows CPC ads.

a. True
b. False

5. AdWords advertisers can benefit from AdSense publishers, and vice versa.

a. True
b. False

Glossary

Above the fold
The information on a web page that is seen before scrolling is necessary.

Account
When signing up for AdWords, users open an account. Accounts contain campaigns.

Ad copy
The words used in an advertisement.

Ad formats
Ad formats include text ads, image ads, video ads, or some combination of all three.

Ad group
An ad group contains one or more ads which are shown in relation to one set of keywords or sites. The advertiser sets a maximum cost-per-click (CPC) or cost-per-thousand-impressions (CPM) for all the keywords or sites in the ad group.

Ad scheduling
Ad scheduling enables AdWords Standard Edition users to control the days and times the ads in their campaigns appear. Users may also choose an advanced mode, which allows them to raise or lower their bids for a campaign at certain times of the day.

Ad unit
A portion of a web page dedicated to an advertisement or group of advertisements.

AdSense
See AdSense for Content and AdSense for Search.

AdSense for Content
Google AdSense method for website publishers to earn money by displaying relevant Google ads on their website's content pages. Because the ads are related to a site's content, they both monetize and enhance the content of the pages.

The program combines pay-per-click and pay-per-impression advertising; site owners get paid for valid clicks on the ads on their site as well as impressions.

AdSense for Search

When website owners place an AdSense search box on their site, they can improve the user's online experience, generate a new revenue stream, and better understand visitors' needs, all at the same time. Site users appreciate the opportunity to search the web from the site, and site owners monetize those searches through clicks on search results pages. The search results pages can be customized to fit any website's theme, and site owners are paid for every valid click on the ads that appear.

Advertising channel

Generally refers to a type of advertising, like AdWords, newspaper, or radio.

AdWords

Google AdWords is a quick and simple way to advertise on Google, regardless of an advertiser's budget. AdWords ads are displayed along with search results on Google, as well as on search and content sites in the growing Google Network, including AOL, EarthLink, HowStuffWorks, & Blogger. Between searches on Google and page views on the Google Network, Google AdWords ads reach a vast audience.

When an advertiser creates an AdWords keyword-targeted ad, the advertiser chooses keywords for which the ad will appear and specifies the maximum amount the advertiser is willing to pay for each click. An advertiser only pays when someone clicks on the ad.

AdWords Discounter

The AdWords Discounter automatically reduces your actual cost-per-click so you pay the lowest price possible for your ad's position on the page (above the next ad).

AdWords Editor

AdWords Editor is a free, downloadable application for managing an AdWords account. Advertisers download their account, makes changes, and then upload the revised campaigns when the changes are finalized.

If an advertiser has a large number of campaigns or keywords, or if an advertiser manages multiple accounts, the AdWords Editor can save time and help streamline workflow. For example, an advertiser can perform detailed searches across campaigns, make multiple changes instantly, and send other people the proposed changes before the changes are posted.

Algorithms

Arithmetic processes or methods used in a larger system.

Animated ad
Graphic advertisements can be still images or animated images.

Auction
AdWords sells the position of an ad to the highest bidder using a modified auction process. Quality Score and maximum CPC (bid) are multiplied to determine ad rank. The AdWords discounter then determines the actual cost-per-click.

Audio Ads
Enables advertisers to target radio listeners by demographic, time of day, or radio station type, for hundreds of radio stations across the U.S. Online reports provide details of when and where ads are played.

Beta test
The final test stage of a product, when it is released to users with certain limitations. Follows an alpha test.

Brand
A brand is a name usually associated with a product or company. Google is a company, but it is also a brand synonymous with search and advertising.

Brand awareness
People's awareness of or ability to quickly recognize a company or product. For example, Google is known for high-quality Internet search.

Branding
The process by which a product or company is associated in advertisements with events, feelings, emotions, or decisions.

Broad match
The default keyword-matching option. If you include general keywords or keyword phrases – such as tennis shoes – in your keyword list, your ads may appear when users search for 'tennis' AND 'shoes', in any order, and possibly along with other terms. For example, your ad may appear for the query buy tennis shoes but not tennis players. Your ads may also appear on relevant variations and pluralized versions of your keyword phrases, as well as on some related keywords and phrases via our expanded keyword matching technology(for instance, in our example, tennis sneakers).

Cache
A temporary computer memory storage area that a web browser or Internet service provider uses to store common pages and graphics that have been recently opened. The cache enables the browser to quickly reload recently viewed pages and images.

'Call' link

When you create a mobile ad, a Call link will appear at the end of your ad text, enabling searchers to connect via phone to your business. Business phone numbers must be domestic, and must not be toll numbers.

Call to action

A direct statement in an ad that tells the user what action they should take immediately. For example, "Make an appointment now."

Campaign

Generally, an effort to reach a target demographic using various advertising media.

An AdWords campaign consists of one or more ad groups. The ads in a given campaign share the same daily budget, language and location targeting, end dates, and syndication options.

Campaign name

Since an AdWords account can contain multiple campaigns, different campaigns can have unique, descriptive names.

Channel

A network or service advertisers use to create online advertisements to be displayed on search engines or other web pages. Google AdWords is a channel. Channels are identified as PPC (pay-per-click) or non-PPC.

Channel type

Channels are identified as PPC (pay-per-click) or non-PPC.

Click-to-call

A link that initiates a phone call between an advertiser and potential customer. The user types in her phone number, and is called by the system. When the user answers the call, the advertiser is then dialed automatically.

Click-through rate

Click-through rate (CTR) is the number of clicks an ad receives divided by the number of times the ad is shown (impressions).

Click-to-play

Users can choose whether to play video ads.

Code snippet

A few lines of software code. For example, with Google AdWords tracking, a small amount of JavaScript code that is added to a specific web page to collect information on how many users see the page.

Content bids

Content bids let AdWords advertisers set one price when their ads run on search sites and a separate price when their ads run on content sites. If an advertiser receives better business leads or a higher ROI from ads on content sites than on search sites (or vice versa), the advertiser can bid more for one kind of site and less for the other. Content bids let advertisers set the prices that are best for their own business.

Advertisers can set content bids for any campaign running on content sites in the Google Network. Content bids are set on the ad group level within each campaign.

Contextual placement

The placement of relevant AdWords ads on content pages in the Google Network.

Conversion

When a user completes an action on an advertiser's site, such as buying something or requesting more information. ("Converting" a visitor to a customer.)

Conversion page

The page where an advertiser confirms that a user has successfully completed a conversion, also called a conversion confirmation page. This is generally the 'Thank you' page appearing after the customer's purchase, subscription, or visit.

Conversion tracking

A free tool from Google to measure conversions and the effectiveness of your AdWords ads and keywords.

Cookie

A small text file downloaded by browser software to a user's computer that can be used to store user information and preferences. Many sites use cookies to customize and improve functionality on repeat visits to a site.

Cost-per-click

The cost-per-click (CPC) is the amount an advertiser pays each time a user clicks on an ad. Google AdWords has a CPC pricing system.

Cost-per-thousand-impressions

With a site-targeted AdWords campaign, the advertiser sets the maximum price to pay for every thousand impressions the advertisement gets on that site. This is called the maximum CPM bid. M is the roman numeral for 1,000.

CPC

Cost-per-click.

CPM
Cost-per-thousand-impressions.

Cross channel conversion tracking
A free tool from Google to analyze all your online advertising channels, such as search, email, and banner ads, through your AdWords account.

Cross segment
A Google Analytics sub-report showing certain types of site performance. For example, reports can be cross-segmented by the city of the visitor, or the keyword that generated a click.

CTR
Click-through rate.

Customized location targeting
Enables advertisers to custom-target ads to specific geographic regions. The user's IP address must be in the designated area in order to see the advertiser's ad.

Daily budget
The amount an advertiser is willing to spend on a specific AdWords campaign each day. AdWords displays an advertiser's ad as often as possible while staying within the advertiser's daily budget. When the budget limit is reached, ads will typically stop showing for that day. How quickly ads are shown during a given day is determined by the ad delivery setting. On any single day, the AdWords system may deliver up to 20% more ads than a daily budget calls for. This helps make up for other days in which a daily budget is not reached. However, an advertiser will never be charged more than an average daily budget over the course of a month. For example: if a daily budget is $10 and the month has 30 days, an advertiser might be charged up to $12 on any single day but monthly charges will never exceed $300.

Differentiating characteristic
A characteristic that can be used to distinguish a product or a company from other products and companies. It is often useful to mention differentiators in ad text.

Display URL
The URL displayed in an ad to tell users to which site they will be taken. Does not need to be the exact same as the destination URL, but it should be an actual URL that is part of the site.

Distribution

The process of displaying ads on various sites.

Distribution preferences

An AdWords advertiser's distribution preference indicates whether the advertiser has chosen to show ads on the search and/or content sites or products (such as blogs or email programs) in the Google Network.

Domains

Website domains are a naming procedure by which web users may identify a particular website address and location (e.g., www.google.com). They are usually made up of two parts: a name and a category. The following are common URL domain categories: .com (commercial), .edu (education), and .gov (government). Domain categories can also be location-specific, for example: .fr (France), .br (Brazil), or .jp (Japan). In some cases, one category is appended to another category, for example: examplename.co.uk, examplename.com.ph, examplename.org.uk.

Domain examples:

* www.google.co.uk*

* www.google.fr

* www.google.com

* www.google.edu

* Domains with the same name but different specific extensions are considered distinct.

End date

Unless an advertiser selects an end date or pauses a campaign, ads will run continuously on Google. Ad campaigns begin at 12:00 AM on the activation date in the time zone the advertiser has chosen for the account, and end at 11:59 PM on the end date chosen by the advertiser.

Exact match keywords

If an advertiser surrounds keywords in brackets (for example [tennis shoes]), ads will appear when users search for the specific phrase ('tennis shoes,' in this case) without any other terms in the query. For example, an ad won't show for the query 'red tennis shoes.' Although an advertiser won't receive as many impressions with exact match, advertisers will likely get a higher click-through rate, because users searching for these terms are typically looking for exactly what is offered.

Expanded text ad

An expanded text ad fills an entire ad unit, rather than being grouped with other text ads. Expanded text ads have the same character limits and editorial guidelines as typical text ads, but are displayed solo and with text enlarged.

Flash

Flash is a plug-in for web browsers enabling viewers to see animation in web page components, including AdWords ads.

Fraud protection

AdWords employs a number of techniques to protect an advertiser's account against invalid activity. Each click on an AdWords ad is examined to filter out potentially invalid clicks. This detection and filtering occurs over a number of levels including the following:

- Real-time systems filter out activity fitting a profile of invalid behavior (such as excessively repetitive clicks)

- Clicks and impressions from known sources of invalid activity are automatically discarded.

GAP

Google Advertising Professional.

Google Advertising Professional

A professional qualification granted to people who have demonstrated expertise with AdWords by passing an exam and managing accounts for a specified time and at a specified spend level.

Google Analytics

Web analytics software is a tool that collects data on website users' behavior.

Google Analytics is a free analytics package that is fully integrated with AdWords. All reports and settings are available from the Analytics tab of an AdWords account.

Google Checkout

Google Checkout makes online shopping quick and easy. Customers can buy items from stores across the web, in just a few steps, sometimes with just one click. This can increase a site's conversion rate.

Google content network

A network of independent websites that show AdWords ads next to the content on their pages.

Google Local Business Center

Advertisers use the Local Business Center to create a free business listing. When potential customers search Google Maps for local information, they'll find the advertiser's business: address, hours of operation, and (optionally) coupons to print out and bring to the advertiser. Business owners don't need a website.

Google Maps

An online mapping tool that can be accessed from a computer or mobile phone.

Google Maps for Mobile

A mapping system optimized for mobile phones and other devices. Users can get real-time traffic information, detailed directions, and local business locations and contact information, all in one integrated map. The interactive maps let users zoom in or out, and move in all directions. Satellite imagery provides a bird's-eye view of a desired location.

Google Network

The Google Network is made up of websites and other products, such as email programs and blogs, which partner with Google to publish AdWords ads.

Google search button

The button on the Google.com web site, toolbar, or third-party site that submits a search term to the Google search engine.

Google search network

The entire collection of Google sites and third-party content sites open for public searching of Internet content.

Google SMS

Google Short Message Service (SMS) enables users to search for certain information from a mobile phone, and returns search results as text messages. Users can get phone book listings, movie show times, weather, facts, dictionary definitions, product prices, and more.

Google Video

An open online video marketplace, where users can search for, watch, and buy TV shows, movies, music videos, documentaries, personal productions, and more.

Headline

In an advertisement, the headline is the main title in the ad.

Host

A server (or servers) or network that provides users with access to digital content and applications.

Image ads
Graphical AdWords ads appearing on select content sites in the Google Network.

Impression
The number of times an ad is displayed on Google or on sites or products in the Google Network. The "Impr" column located on your reporting statistics page refers to the number of "impressions" for your ad.

Inactive for search
A keyword is assigned the status of 'inactive for search' and stops triggering ads because its maximum CPC bid doesn't meet or exceed the minimum CPC bid required to be eligible to compete in the auction. This minimum CPC bid is based on a keyword's Quality Score.

Index
The search-engine database against which searchers can query. With "crawler based" search engines, the index typically copies of all the web pages found by automatically "crawling" (searching) the web. With human-powered directories, the index contains the summaries of all websites that have been categorized.

Information window
The balloon that appears on Google Maps displaying a local business ad.

In-stream video ads
A video ad shown in the middle of a video.

Keyword
The keywords an advertiser chooses for a given ad group are used to target their ads to potential customers. Keywords are also what a searcher enters into a search engine when trying to find information.

Keyword match types
Search-targeted keywords can be specified as broad matches, phrase matches, exact matches, or negative matches. It is recommended to use a combination of two or more of these techniques to run an effective ad campaign.

Keyword targeting
A type of AdWords campaign where the advertiser selects keywords that will trigger ads from the campaign. Keyword-targeted ads can appear on search results pages, on content pages, and on other properties on the Google Network.

Keyword status

A keyword's status reflects whether it is eligible to enter the ad auction and trigger ads. Each keyword, except for negative keywords, can have a performance classification of either 'Active' or 'Inactive for search'. Keywords are also subject to review by AdWords; if keywords don't comply with editorial guidelines, they will be disapproved.

Language targeting

When determining where to show your ads, the AdWords system looks at a user's language preference (set via the 'Preferences' link next to the Search Bar on the Google homepage) to see if it matches one of the languages that your campaign targets. For example, users whose Google language preference is Spanish will see ads in campaigns targeted to Spanish.

Each Google domain's language setting defaults to the language most commonly associated with that Google domain. For example, Google.com defaults to English, Google.fr defaults to French, etc.

Lifetime customer value

The total amount spent by a customer over all transactions. While the cost of a customer acquisition may be higher than the value of the first sale, subsequent transactions may make that customer profitable by many times more than the cost of acquiring the customer.

Local business ad

An AdWords ad associated with a business listing on Google Maps.

Location targeting

AdWords advertisers can specify a geographic location within which to display ads. Ads will be shown to users who search Google Maps in that location using that advertiser's keywords. They will also be shown to users anywhere who specify a region in the wording of their searches that matches the advertiser's location target.

Marketing mix

The blend of product, place, promotion, and pricing strategies designed to produce satisfying exchanges with a target market.

Max CPC

Maximum cost-per-click.

Maximum cost per click

An advertiser's maximum cost-per-click (CPC) is the highest amount that an advertiser is willing to pay for a click on an ad. An advertiser can set a maximum CPC at the keyword or ad group level. The AdWords Discounter automatically reduces the amount so that the actual CPC that an advertiser is charged is just one cent more than the minimum necessary to keep the ad positioned above the next lower ad on the page.

Maximum CPM

Maximum cost-per-thousand-impressions. The maximum CPM (or max CPM) is set by advertisers who run site-targeted ads. Max CPM is the greatest amount they are willing to pay for each 1000 impressions their ad receives on the targeted sites they select. Because of the auction system, advertisers pay less than their max CPM.

Metrics

For websites, data that is collected regarding site usage. Examples include number of page views, the total number of purchases made through a site, and the number of click-throughs that resulted from an advertisement.

Minimum CPC bid

The amount assigned to a given keyword based on its quality (or Quality Score). The minimum bid is the least that an advertiser must bid to compete in the auction. Actual CPC may be lower.

Mobile ads

Mobile ads are short, text-based AdWords ads that appear when users search Google from a mobile phone or device. When clicked on, users can be directed to your mobile web page or can be automatically connected to a business phone.

Mobile markup language

A markup language, such as HTML, has codes for indicating layout and styling. Websites that are designed for viewing on mobile devices use a mobile markup language.

Monetize

(In the context of a website) To make money from advertising or other activities.

Navigation

Describes the movement of a user through a website or other application interface. User navigation refers to the system of available links and buttons available to navigate through the website.

Negative-match keywords

Advertisers can use negative keywords to prevent ads from showing in relation to irrelevant searches. To specify a negative keyword, place a negative sign (-) before the keyword. If the keyword is 'tennis shoes' and an advertiser adds the negative keyword '-cheap,' the ad won't appear when a user searches for 'cheap tennis shoes.' Advertisers can apply this option for a keyword at both the ad group and campaign level.

Opening image

The static image that is displayed for a video ad. When a user clicks the opening image or the play button, the video component of the ad will be played.

Optimization

Optimization is the process of modifying ad campaigns to improve the quality and performance of AdWords ads.

PageRank™

Google's patented method for measuring page importance on a scale from 0 to 10, where 10 is most important. The PageRank™ algorithm analyzes the quality and quantity of links that point to a page.

Pay-per-action

As opposed to pay-per-click advertising, pay-per-action ads incur a charge after generating a specific action, such as a purchase or a subscription to a newsletter.

Phrase match keywords

If a keyword is entered into the AdWords system in quotation marks, e.g. "tennis shoes", ads will appear when a user searches for the words 'tennis shoes' in this order. The search can also contain other terms as long as it includes the exact phrase specified. For example, in this case, an ad may appear for the queries 'buy tennis shoes' and 'tennis shoes store' but not 'shoes for tennis.'

Pixel

The smallest part of a digital image.

Play rate

The 'play rate' column in video-ad reports indicates the number of plays a video received divided by the number of times the video ad was shown (impressions).

Position preference
Position preference enables advertisers to specify which ad position an ad will show in among all the ads on a given page. For example, if an advertiser finds that an ad gets the best results when it is positioned third or fourth among all AdWords ads, the advertiser can set a position preference for those spots. Separate position preferences can be set for any or all of the keywords in a campaign.

Pricing model
The method used to determine how much a product costs.

Print ads
Advertisements printed in newspapers, magazines, or other printed circulations

Publishers
The people or organizations that publish the advertisement.

Quality Score
Quality Score is the basis for measuring the quality and relevance of ads in relation to a specific keyword. Quality Score determines your minimum CPC. Factors included in this score include a keyword's click-through rate and the relevance of a) ad text, b) keywords, and c) the landing page users are sent to when they click on the ad.

Query
A word, phrase, or group of words used to seek information from a search engine. Also, the act of performing a search.

Rank
AdWords rank is the process that determines in which position an ad will be shown (rank is not synonymous with position). Rank = CPC X Quality Score.

Reach
People who see an advertisement were "reached."

Referring source
Referrer; the URL of an HTML page that refers visitors to a site.

Relevance
Relevance refers to the usefulness of information (such as an ad or a landing page) to a user. Relevance, or the quality of an ad, is reflected by a keyword's Quality Score.

Return on ad spend (ROAS)
A measurement of how much revenue a company generated from specific sales compared to how much was spent on the ad campaign driving those sales. See ROI.

Return on investment (ROI)
ROI (Return on Investment) = (Revenue - Cost)/ Cost, expressed as a percentage.

ROAS
Return on ad spend.

ROI
Return on investment.

SafeSearch
A user setting that, when enabled, filters out certain results. For example, if SafeSearch is on, adult advertising or other content inappropriate for children will not appear in the search results.

Search Engine Marketing
The process of targeting advertisements to specific search results.

Search result
A web page or other item found by a search engine for a given search term. The first item is the most relevant match found, the second is the next most relevant, and so on. Clicking on any underlined item will take a user to the associated web page.

Search results page
The web page returned containing the ranked search results.

SEM
Search Engine Marketer or Search Engine Marketing.

Shopping cart abandonment
When a potential customer puts an item or items in an e-commerce shopping cart, but does not complete the transaction.

Similar Pages
When Google returns search results, often it includes a "Similar Pages" link under each result. This link returns another page of search results, similar to the one to which the link is attached.

Site exclusion tool
The site exclusion tool allows advertisers to refine targeting of their ads on the content network by preventing specific websites from showing certain ads.

Site sections

Where advertisements for specific products or services appear on a site. Can comprise only one section or even one page of a site. If a merchant is advertising soccer shoes, for instance, he might choose to advertise only on the sports section of a news site rather than placing ads across the entire site. In the example below, ads could be targeted to the section or subsection level.

example.com/section/subsection/

Site targeted

A campaign in which the advertiser selects the individual websites in the Google content network on which ads will appear.

Source

In the context of campaign tracking, a source is the origin of a referral. Examples of sources are the Google search engine, a link in a newsletter, or the URL of a referring website.

Sponsored Links

A designator indicating ads (as opposed to natural search results) on a search results page.

Stream

Data transmission (such as video) that occurs in a continuous flow. Streaming video files enable you to play the beginning before all the data has been delivered.

Target

Ad campaigns can generally be targeted by language and location.

Total value

The total value generated by conversions of a specific tracking type.

Tracking URL

URLs appended with parameters that, when clicked on, provide information about the source of the click, the search query used, and other advertising metrics. Tracking URLs help advertisers determine the effectiveness of their ads and/or keywords on non-AdWords channels.

For example, if a URL is www.somedomain.com, the tracking URL could be www.somedomain.com/?source=googleadwords.

Tracking URL parameters

See Tracking URL.

Transaction

A single occurrence of a conversion event, for example a sale.

Uniform Resource Locator (URL)

The address/location of a web page or file on the Internet.

Unique visitors

People who come to a website for the first time and have not accessed the site before.

URL

Uniform Resource Locator.

User preferences (on google.com)

Enables users to set a preferred interface language, filter search results, and other functions.

Users

The people or customers who "use" a search engine or website or read an advertisement.

Video ad

When an AdWords video ad is shown, it is displayed as a static opening image. The user must click on the image for the video to play. If the user clicks on the video as it is playing, he or she will be taken to the web page linked to from the video.

Video feed

On the Internet, a video available from a source such as a camera at a live event or server.

Web analytics software

Software that aggregates website traffic information such as which links were visited most often, how many times an item was downloaded, and so forth. The software usually displays site usage statistics and patterns in graphs. The data can then be used to better manage the site, adjust marketing, and refine the business.